MANAGING EMPLOYEE PERFORMANCE PROBLEMS

by

Neville C. Tompkins

THOMSON

NETg

CREDITS
Product Manager: *Debbie Woodbury*
Managing Editor: *Kathleen Barcos*
Editor: *Kay Keppler*
Typesetting: *ExecuStaff*
Cover Design: *David Newman*

For more information contact:

NETg
25 Thomson Place
Boston, MA 02210

Or find us on the Web at **www.courseilt.com**

For permission to use material from this text or product, submit a request online at www.thomsonrights.com.

© 1997 by NETg, a division of Thomson Learning. Thomson Learning is a trademark used herein under license.
Printed in the United States of America

 6 7 8 9 10 08 07 06

Library of Congress Catalog Card Number 97-65302
Tompkins, Neville C.
Managing Employee Performance Problems
ISBN 10: 1-56052-428-6
ISBN 13: 978-1-56052-428-1

CONTENTS

F O R E W O R D

This book crystallizes my experience in helping hundreds of line and staff managers sort out work performance problems with employees at all levels of an organization.

The book is intended to be a practical document with a minimum of psychological introspection and a maximum of hands-on information for the line or staff manager to consider when facing a deterioration of job performance by an employee. I don't claim to have all the answers, but I have tried to focus on what works in improving situations of work performance decline.

The fact sheets on performance problems outlined in Chapter 5 have been developed largely from my experience as a corporate human resources manager. As a double check I asked business friends and peers in line and staff positions to review my perspective. For these second opinions I am indebted to Bob Adams, Dan Ames, Vickie Cortese, Bill Neal, Al Orheim, Garry Ritzky, Kenny Sawyer, John Smoyer, and Susanne Taylor.

The American Health Association, National Business Coalition for AIDS, and the National Council for Alcoholism and Drug Dependency supplied helpful background information.

RESPONSIBILITIES

CHAPTER 1

MANAGING EMPLOYEES TODAY

Every hour of every workday managers carry out a very important, but often regarded as a negative, part of the job. This is to provide guidance, redirection, counseling, or discipline to an employee.

These business managers are the manufacturing supervisors, sales office managers, technical or project leaders, or the president or chief executive officer of their firms. Their task is to get the job done on time and within budget constraints and to meet a particular delivery schedule or service need of the employer.

To a large extent, managers accomplish their jobs through people—the men and women who report to them. Managers delegate duties and responsibilities, train new employees, retrain those who need it, orient new hires, encourage and reward those who perform well, and redirect, discipline, and even terminate those who do not meet job performance requirements. It's all part of the job of managing, and not every manager does it well. Some shy away from performance problems and do nothing about the deterioration in job performance; others need guidance and help from upper-level managers or human resource professionals so that they carry out their responsibility of improving job performance.

Little is static in today's business or service environment. Organizations that continue to operate as they did 20 or 30 years ago are not likely to survive, because the global economy moves quickly, continually raising the standards of performance and innovation for employers and employees. If one company doesn't change, its competitor will, seizing opportunities and ultimately customers and clients. The "good old days" are increasingly only memories, the way things used to be.

In some modern settings, employee teams carry out many managerial roles with the supervisor operating more as a facilitator, helper, and educator of the work team. Many of these self-empowered activities work well, but in most American organizations, a manager is still called on to lead the work group, to hold them responsible for the work produced or the service provided, and to guide, redirect, retrain, and as necessary, discipline members of the work group.

The Changing Workforce

The U.S. workforce and its attitude toward work has changed markedly in the last 30 years. Women have entered the labor force in greater numbers, and there are more single-parent and dual-earner families than ever before. Men are assuming greater responsibilities in the home for child care and the care of elderly or infirm family members.

I have written this book to help managers define and resolve the kinds of problems that arise when people go to work. The center section provides fact sheets to guide supervisors in managing employee performance in dozens of situations encountered from time to time in a manager's worklife. Resolving employee issues may not be easy, but it can be rewarding—for you, for the worker, and for the company.

The New Supervisor

The transition from worker to boss is not always easy. Newly appointed managers need to acquire new roles—changing from a doer to a person who leads the doers, delegates assignments to others, and holds them responsible for the work.

Newly appointed managers now have authority and power to use in the supervision of their people, and if they use it judiciously, they will gain acceptance in their new role. They will have to make decisions affecting work and people, and they will have to solve problems, including employee performance problems. They will initiate corrective action and perhaps discipline people, some of whom were formerly co-workers. They must now remember what motivated them as workers to produce good work.

The transition from worker to supervisor may be awkward. It's difficult at times to supervise one's friends. Supervisors inevitably must take actions that don't mix well with friendship. The front office says that managers must be consistent in their decisions and fair, treating everyone the way they would like to be treated. Those are good words, but not always easy to implement.

Handling interpersonal difficulties is part of the job of managing. Managing means meeting unit goals and objectives through strong job performance or correcting employee work habits so that workers can improve performance and meet goals.

Handling Employee Complaints

Part of the job of managing is listening to employee questions, concerns, and complaints; investigating them; and doing something about legitimate matters. That role is important because employee dissatisfaction over concerns and complaints, if left unresolved or unanswered, can lead to employee dissatisfaction and affect job performance.

Sometimes questions, concerns, or complaints arise only because the employee doesn't know or understand company policies and procedures or specific job requirements. This lack of information can make employees feel insecure and lead to lowered morale and productivity. Job training, retraining, or a good orientation process for new employees can help reduce the number of these concerns and get the employee productive more quickly.

Resolving complaints can be time consuming. Once managers have heard an employee complaint, they should investigate and respond to it. This may take time as the manager contacts other departments in the company to obtain the needed information. If the supervisor's response is negative, then more time may be required to explain it to the employee and try to get the person back on even keel.

Employee complaints or grievances take on a special value with immediate supervisors. Often these complaints are a challenge to the existing system—company policies or procedures, work procedures, supervisory techniques—and make it difficult at times for the supervisor to keep an objective posture. But that's part of a manager's job—to listen, investigate, return with a report, and convey it to the employee and still retain that employee's goodwill for the longer pull.

CONFLICT—AN OPPORTUNITY FOR GROWTH

When two or more persons come together on the job with different ideas, opinions, work experiences, or educational backgrounds, there is an opportunity for smooth and cooperative endeavor—or for conflict.

Cooperation, the art of working well together, makes the manager's job easier, but not all conflict is bad. Managed conflict can be the basis of greater personal understanding, more focused job goals, and greater productivity and profit. However, unmanaged conflict can affect job performance negatively.

Conflict should never be allowed to fester. This is a manager's responsibility—to determine the depth and breadth of the problem, bring the parties together to air their views and concerns, and compare those to company policies and work procedures (or a common-sense approach) to overcome performance problems.

It's best to try to allow the disputing parties to work out their own problems, but at times the manager, as the ranking company representative in the discussions, may have to take the lead role and lay down job performance requirements. Then he or she must follow up to be sure that the resolution or company procedures have been implemented.

Growing on the Job

Workers are hired to fill a specific need. However, a job should provide a worker with more than a paycheck and benefits—a job should offer an opportunity for personal growth.

A person hired into a labor pool in a factory, for example, may have an interest in becoming a machine operator and, in time, a maintenance mechanic. An office secretary may be perfectly satisfied to be a secretary and rise through those ranks; others have their eyes on administrative assistants' jobs or seek to climb one of the many career ladders in modern offices—perhaps as a credit analyst, an interviewer in the human resources department, an expediter in the purchasing organization, or as a scheduler in the production planning group.

Personal growth is often achieved by climbing the career ladder in one company. If career growth is not available in one organization, an employee may move on to try to achieve it in another company.

Helping employees achieve their goals is another managerial responsibility, and one that sometimes requires sensitivity and problem-solving skills. Most managers and supervisors accept their basic responsibilities of managing and want to help employees. They try to correct job performance problems of those who report to them.

Employment At Will

Employment at will means that an employee is not bound to stay with the employer forever and the employer may terminate the employee at any time. A few organizations make no effort to correct or redirect work performance and summarily dismiss an employee who does not achieve accepted work standards, making use of the employment-at-will concept in its broadest context.

Under the common law theory of employment at will, the employer has no constraints and has the right to hire, fire, demote, and promote whomever they choose for any reason, unless there is a contract (such as a union agreement) or federal, state, or local law to the contrary. Some states have also generated legal limits on what employers may do in hiring and firing.

Many employers maintain an employment-at-will status so that in the event of a business decline the workforce can be adjusted as needed to meet business conditions. Such a "management right" also allows a fair employer to terminate for cause and discipline as needed to keep positive morale in the workforce.

Managers should be trained not to use language with workers that suggests employment is secure for any specified period of time. The term "permanent employee" should be dropped from the vocabulary in favor of terms such as "regular employee," "temporary worker," or "part-time employee."

Resolving Difficult Situations

Many of the conflict situations that a manager faces can be resolved relatively quickly—redirection of employee efforts at the work station, perhaps a short meeting or a counseling or disciplinary session.

But some of the intense problems of the modern workplace are not so easily resolved—drug use at work, violence in the workplace, a serious job injury, a police investigation of an employee, or a government investigation of work practices at the company.

These unusual incidents will require a supervisor's time, patience, and often guidance from upper management or the human resources or legal departments. But the experience and common sense of the supervisor should allow him or her to manage these tense situations effectively, drawing on upper level or professional assistance as needed.

Sometimes supervisors have to manage difficult employees. Some of these employees would dominate co-workers and even the supervisor if allowed. Some never speak up or only rarely give feedback. Some find something wrong with every request that is made. Some are chronic complainers. Many of these situations are discussed in the fact sheets included in Chapter 5.

CARRYING OUT DECISIONS LEGALLY AND FAIRLY

Modern business has no place for the managerial gunslinger who goes about job duties with little regard for others. These days federal, state, and local laws, union contracts and company policies guide managers on how they are expected to carry out job responsibilities. In many organizations formal training programs help managers gain a level of comfort to carry out these responsibilities effectively.

Many company policies call for progressive discipline of employees, unless the facts of the situation warrant immediate suspension or termination. Even if termination appears to be warranted, wise management policies will often call for a suspension, sometimes with pay, so that adequate time is allowed to investigate the matter, interview witnesses, assess the relative importance of the violation, review the proposed action with upper management, and advise the employee accordingly.

Managers have a responsibility to carry out employment decisions legally and fairly. Legally means that the intended employment action meets requirements of the law, any union contract, and any formal or informal company policies. Fairly means that the employee is treated the way the supervisor would like to be treated or the way the supervisor would treat the majority of employees in the work unit. Historical treatment of workers can also be a factor if the employee protests treatment not usually applied to others.

Managers face many challenges in today's workplace. In the next chapter we will discuss a manager's rights and responsibilities in managing and some of the types of issues faced by a busy manager in greater detail.

CHAPTER

RIGHTS AND RESPONSIBILITIES IN MANAGING

The job of a manager or supervisor is to produce a product or provide a service and, in most situations, to do that through people—the employees and other workers.

Some managers are experts in a particular phase of the business; as engineers, scientists, or accountants they may work alone and supervise no other persons. But usually the more important role of a manager is to see that results are achieved through people. The manager's technical expertise should be used to guide the employee in successful completion of work assignments. Technical expertise is important, but it is people expertise that is often lacking.

The challenge is to get the supervisor or manager to manage their employees legally, fairly, and with confidence. Techniques will vary with each employee, from the new hire during an orientation period to the respected worker whose performance is declining because of boredom on the job. Successful job performance involves setting clear performance standards, evaluating employee work efforts against those standards, appreciating and encouraging above-average performance, and counseling and redirecting those who fall below expected or required performance levels.

Resolving workplace friction is one of the most important roles of the immediate supervisor. If conflict is overcome by good working relationships, then productivity and morale is enhanced. Conflict and discord, if not managed well, can result in deteriorating morale, complaints, grievances, dissatisfaction, and turnover.

Employee Questions, Concerns, and Complaints

Employees will have questions about company policies, concerns about their work environment, and, at times, legitimate complaints about work conditions, company policies, or treatment on the job by a supervisor or a co-worker.

Employees have a basic right to air their concerns to their immediate supervisor or company representative. Employees who are not permitted to air their concerns to management can become angry or depressed; when morale suffers, productivity and product quality can suffer. Some government laws give workers the right to speak up about specific conditions in the workplace or the method of treatment on the job.

Other government laws give employees the right to complain and to engage in what is called *concerted activity* to emphasize a complaint. These are *protected complaints,* since federal and state laws banning discrimination not only protect those who complain about discrimination they may have suffered but also those who cooperate in the investigation of a complaint or who testify in agency or court proceedings. Whenever employees band together to protest wages or working conditions, they are engaged in protected, concerted activity under federal labor law.

There are limits to employee protests and complaints. How a protest is lodged and what it pertains to frequently determine whether the action is protected. The law doesn't prohibit an employer from taking legitimate disciplinary action for unacceptable work performance against someone who has filed a complaint. But be aware that any action taken that is detrimental to the employee or that might be construed to be a departure from traditional employment practices can be suspect.

Managers need input from company human resource managers and legal counsel so that they do not take inappropriate disciplinary action in such cases.

Harnessing and Directing Employee Emotions

Employee emotions and feelings—fear, joy, excitement, frustration, sadness, anxiety, elation—come into the work place every day with the employee. The challenge for the manager or supervisor is to understand the emotions and what to do about them. When understood and managed wisely, emotions can enhance a business success. If they go unacknowledged, are misunderstood, or mismanaged, they can set a business back.

Positive emotions can help teams work better together, create commitment and excitement about work, energize workers, and help them unleash their creativity. Workplace emotions, unleashed and misdirected, can result in conflict at the job site.

Most workers want to do a good job. The more information they have about the company, the work unit, and its objectives, the better they are able to mount a work effort that pays off in higher productivity and better quality. Workers with emotional problems that outweigh job performance needs will drag down their own productivity and often have a negative effect on co-workers' morale and productivity.

EMPLOYEE JOB PERFORMANCE: THE REAL BALL GAME

Many activities in the work environment can distract employees from their jobs. Personal health concerns, family worries, and petty envies and jealousies about other workers can divert employee attention from producing a quality product or providing a service on time within cost parameters. For that reason, the thrust of a supervisor's direction and follow-up actions should be aimed at improving job performance.

Confidentiality and Employee Privacy

Experienced supervisors who see an employee's job performance declining may ask a very normal question: "What's wrong?" That question may help provide the answer to get the employee back on track and producing well again.

13

But be careful. There is fine line between being friendly and helpful to an employee and crossing over into matters the employee may consider to be private and personal. Similarly, supervisors may become aware of personal information about the employee that they do not need to know; such information should *not* be introduced in discussions with the employee. If the employee presents the information or raises the issue, the supervisor may be able to assist, but the manager should not ask for private information directly.

RESOLVING WORKPLACE CONFLICT

One of the most import leadership roles of a supervisor is resolving workplace conflict as it arises. Not every employee comes to work every day full of enthusiasm, raring to get at the job and produce superior results.

Family concerns, personal health worries, problems with commuting, and disputes with co-workers can pull down even the most hardy worker. That's why leadership qualities of a supervisor are so important—to sense those areas of potential conflict, investigate, bring the disputing parties together, sort out the reasons, and redirect employees so that they can get on with the job.

Resolving workplace conflict does not require a dictatorial approach. Supervisors should take the time to talk to people—to investigate—and set up the necessary preventive actions to avoid a repeat of the situation, including, if necessary, counseling and disciplinary actions. Solving the problem should be the thrust of the supervisor's efforts.

Complaining vs. Insubordination

There is fine line between an employee complaining legitimately and insubordination or refusal to perform assigned tasks. An employee who airs a complaint but carries out assigned work is not guilty of insubordination. However, if an employee's outburst directly undermines a supervisor's authority, the behavior may be insubordinate.

Generally, employees are required to "obey now, grieve later" when it comes to complaints about work assignments or other employment decisions. They can't hide behind a complaint to dodge their work responsibilities. However, workers can refuse an assignment if they feel that doing the work would endanger their or their co-workers' health and safety.

No retaliation!   Several government laws prohibit company repre-sentatives from taking retaliatory action against employees who expose corrupt, illegal, or prohibited workplace activities and actions. Supervi-sors need to be trained in the basics of these employment laws, because "whistleblowers" are told at the outset that they may file a claim without fear of retaliation by their employer. If retaliation should occur and be proved, the employer—and the supervisor—will face further government scrutiny and charges. Even if the initial complaint turns out to be groundless, any retaliatory action by the employer could lead to a law-suit by the complainer.

Supervisors who fear that whistleblowers will charge them with retaliation should consult with their human resources manager for guidance. As difficult as it may be, supervisors should try to treat the employee as if nothing happened. Supervisors should not feel hand-cuffed in dealings with the employee, but they should be careful in their dealings. Any actions taken, particularly any that might be considered adverse to the employee, should be reviewed by another manager and documented so that the supervisor can establish legitimate business reasons for the action.

The manager should be able to show that:

- The behavior of the individual violates company policy or government law

- The employee has been made aware of the policy and the consequences of violations through orientation, training, and communication

- The action proposed is consistent with actions taken in the past for similar offenses

- Company records show a legitimate, nondiscriminatory reason for the action.

Conducting An Investigation

The easiest part of a supervisor's job is when the employee is forth-right and tells the supervisor what's wrong. That allows the supervisor to deal directly with the employee, counseling, correcting, redirecting, or assisting as needed.

Sometimes the office grapevine will suggest reasons for the person's abnormal behavior. Such commentary should not be accepted at face value but used as a starting point to suggest possible reasons for the behavior. Supervisors should then dig deeper, endeavoring to isolate the reasons for the unusual behavior that is affecting work performance.

Resolving workplace conflict involves separating people from the issues involved and handling each effectively. Empathetic listening will help a lot, allowing workers to vent and permitting the supervisor to bring the conversation around to resolving the work issues involved.

Investigations on these matters should involve only those with a need to know—perhaps upper level managers, the human resources professional, the occupational health staff, or persons who can contribute understanding for the behavior. All others should be left out—don't make anyone's behavior a topic of gossip in the department or work area.

Adjusting Supervisory Style

Sometimes managers can correct employee performance problems by adjusting their style of supervision with that particular employee.

Some shop floor workers look to their supervisors for detailed, specific instructions on what to do. Other employees may be more effective when given a free rein within the framework of the company policies to get the job done. Close supervision of those who don't like it will stifle natural efforts to get the job done well. In both of these situations, managers should consider adjusting their supervisor style to the work style of the employee.

CORRECTIVE ACTIONS

Once a supervisor has found the reason for a person's nonproductive behavior, it is time to take corrective action, which may involve counseling, reinstruction in job duties, redirection of work efforts, a change of assignment or shift, or a regrouping of co-workers.

Some incidents may be closed with one direct, single corrective action before the employee is back performing at his or her former level of performance. In more complex situations, corrective actions may require some time and several meetings to provide the sustained redirection of work efforts required.

Discipline and Termination Procedures

Most organizations have established procedures to handle errant employees where basic efforts at correction go unheeded. If counseling and cautions haven't worked, then more serious and formal procedures may have to be taken.

Some firms institute *progressive discipline,* unless the facts of the case warrant immediate suspension or termination. In progressive discipline, steps may begin with verbal warnings or counseling and progress to written warnings, suspensions from work (with or without pay), "last chance letters," and finally termination.

In unionized organizations, the labor contract usually calls for the presence of a union steward in serious disciplinary sessions to represent the employee. In nonunion settings it is advisable to have another supervisor or a human resource representative present as a management witness in serious disciplinary interviews.

Not every person is suited for work at every company nor is compatible with the culture, goals and objectives, and policies of every company. Some persons simply will not fit, and the sooner it is realized by both parties, the sooner the trouble can and should end.

Avoiding Workplace Discrimination

Discrimination charges are far more likely to be filed over promotion and termination policies than hiring decisions. That means that present or former employees are more likely to file a discrimination charge than applicants who were denied a job.

Employees are protected by a broad range of federal and state antidiscrimination laws. Federal law, for example, prohibits discrimination against any person age 40 or over in employment. Some state statutes go further, prohibiting discrimination against persons on the job of any age. Managers should be aware that the 1991 expansion of Title VII of the Civil Rights Act expands employee rights allowing for jury trials and punitive damages, in addition to back pay, for victims of job discrimination. The Americans with Disabilities Act (ADA) prohibits discrimination against persons with disabilities.

Conduct formal, written performance evaluations regularly. It's harder to defend a discrimination complaint when the employee's personnel file is empty—or worse—when it contains a series of glowing performance reviews.

Here are questions that should be asked in any termination decision:

- Do you have an objective, documented reason for the decision?
- Could an employee reasonably claim that the decision runs afoul of any fair employment law?
- Does the decision create a perception of unfairness or discrimination?

The key question often raised in the minds of jurors as they deliberate a case is: "Did the employer treat the person fairly?"

Solving the Problem Is a Manager's Responsibility

Managers by the very nature of their titles are problem solvers—or should be. When a worker has a problem that affects work performance, the manager should be interested and get involved. At times the supervisor's patience will be tried, but he or she should try to set aside personal feelings to work through the problem with the employee.

The manager should try to define the issue, investigate the circumstances, take appropriate corrective action, and follow through to see that the corrective action is working. That sounds like a simple formula and, if carefully followed, it can work.

CHAPTER

3

RIGHTS AND RESPONSIBILITIES OF EMPLOYEES

Labor laws are on the books of federal, state, and local governments for one principal purpose— to protect employees. These laws affect the day-to-day operation of a business, the techniques that managers use in supervising their people, and the employees who work at the company.

Managers and supervisors have a legal responsibility to be aware of these laws and to apply them in dealings with their workers. Some laws also require the employer to post public notices to inform employees of regulations that affect them, or, where specifically required, to train employees in the details of the regulation.

Supervisors need to be trained in the details of these laws and most human resource managers have full text copies of the acts on hand for easy reference.

When line and staff managers understand the applicable regulations, they will gain the confidence and authority to guide the organization along the path of compliance. They should know who is covered by the law, the enforcement agency, any exemptions under the law, the range of penalties, and the statute of limitations for filing a claim.

Ignorance of the law is not an acceptable reason to violate it. The watchword for managers should be: Stay informed!

Federal Laws

Many federal laws govern the relationship between manager and worker. These laws include wage and hour regulations, which specify how workers will be paid and when they are entitled to overtime. Antidiscrimination laws have been enacted, with the Equal Employment Opportunity Commission (EEOC) acting as the principal enforcement agency for violations of laws against race, sex, age, and disability discrimination.

Protection and safety for workers on the job has been enacted under the Occupational Safety and Health Act (OSHA), and employers can expect unannounced visits from OSHA compliance officers in response to employee complaints and for programmed inspections in high hazard industries.

State and Local Laws

Where the federal government may have stopped passing labor laws, states, counties, and cities have enacted laws of their own. There is a good measure of duplication between federal laws and some state and local statutes.

Some states have gone beyond the federal law by enacting their own laws in areas such as discrimination, safety and health, and other areas. For example, while OSHA has been trying to enact an indoor air law for commercial buildings, many states have partially filled the void and enacted restricted smoking laws.

Managers should realize that a federal law such as the Americans with Disabilities Act (ADA) preempts state and local laws only if federal regulations provide benefits in excess of the state or local law. Otherwise, that segment of the local law that is more protective of the employee remains in effect.

Rights of Employees

Some federal laws spell out what a worker should do if he or she feels aggrieved by a management action. Most of these laws are slanted towards the worker to provide job and safety protection for the employee.

But that is not always the case. A balanced view of employee and management rights and responsibilities is outlined in the OSHA information booklet (#2056) entitled *All About OSHA*.

OSHA says that it does not cite employees for violations of their responsibilities, but points out that each employee "shall comply with all occupational safety and health standards and all rules, regulations, and orders issued under the Act" that are applicable. OSHA outlines these employee rights:

- Employees have a right to seek safety and health on the job without fear of punishment

- Employees shall not be punished or discriminated against for complaining to an employer, union, OSHA, or other government agency about job safety and health hazards, or for filing safety and health grievances

- Employees shall not be discriminated against for participating in a workplace safety and health committee or participating in OSHA conferences or hearings.

Safety is not a one-way ticket. In addition to employee rights, OSHA outlines these employee responsibilities:

- Read the OSHA poster at the worksite

- Comply with all applicable OSHA standards

- Follow all employer safety and health rules and regulations, and wear or use prescribed protective equipment while engaged in work

- Report hazardous conditions to the supervisor

- Report any job-related injury or illness to the employer and seek treatment promptly

- Cooperate with the OSHA compliance officer conducting an inspection if he or she inquires about safety and health conditions in the workplace.

Other federal and state regulations have similar balances. For example, the ADA requires employers to provide "reasonable accommodation" to workers with recognized disabilities as long as the worker can perform the essential functions of the job, the job is not a hazard to the employee or co-workers, and the cost of the accommodation is not an "undue burden" to the employer.

HOW TO COMPLAIN EFFECTIVELY

There are many ways for a worker to raise questions with management or to formally complain about a workplace condition or supervisory treatment. Employees in a union can file a written grievance, or employees can complain to OSHA, which may result in having an OSHA compliance officer inspect the facility. Employees can write an anonymous complaint to the president of the company, or, if they feel aggrieved under a federal or state law, they can file a complaint with the EEOC.

Any employee—even a supervisor complaining to higher levels of management—has a right to complain, but there are effective ways to get a fair hearing. Here are steps to get an effective hearing:

- The employee should discuss the matter with the immediate supervisor or the manager who took what the employee believes is adverse action against him or her. That manager or supervisor needs to hear directly from the employee about his or her concern, the reasons for the concern, and what redress the employee seeks.

- Unless the grievance is an emergency or life-threatening situation that demands the supervisor's immediate attention, the employee should ask to speak to the supervisor on a day and time when he or she can give undivided attention to the worker. With that type of consideration, the employee is more likely to get a full hearing.

- The supervisor may ask for time to investigate. That time should be provided willingly by the employee. In turn, the employee has the right to expect to hear back from the supervisor in due course. If the investigation is delayed, the employee should be so informed—and a new date set for the response. In the process, the supervisor may introduce other specialists or experts to assist in the investigation or explanation—the supervisor's immediate manager or persons from the human resources or payroll department, benefits specialists, etc.

■ The supervisor should be prepared to provide a full explanation as to why the employee's complaint has been resolved favorably— the reasons why and when the remedial action will be taken.

If the supervisor must decline the request, then the employee is also entitled to hear the reasons why and the company policy or procedure or state or federal law that must be followed in the decision. In some cases it may be appropriate to outline the reasons for rejecting the complaint in writing to allow time for the employee to digest the supervisor's words.

■ If the employee is still not satisfied with the immediate supervisor's response, permit him or her to appeal the decision to the supervisor's manager, the human resources department, or even the ranking company manager. Some companies have a corporate ombudsman who is the final level of appeal after all other internal avenues of remedy have been exhausted.

Some organizations have established an alternate dispute resolution (ADR) procedure at the time of hiring, where new employees agree to exhaust internal complaint procedures and then go to mediation session, often chaired by trained co-workers who hear the dispute and administer a binding ruling. Employees dissatisfied with the internal mediation process may then go to external agencies such as the EEOC, but employers who have used the ADR process find that the number of complaints to these government agencies declines markedly when an effective ADR process is used in the company.

AN EMPLOYEE'S PRIVACY RIGHTS

The U.S. Supreme Court has said that although employees have a right to privacy in the workplace, that right is not absolute. The law says that employees have a "reasonable expectation of privacy," but what is "reasonable" is determined almost in a case-by-case situation.

For example, the company gives an employee a desk, which is company property; therefore, the employer has an interest that the desk is used for legitimate purposes. However, if the employer says the

Qualities Employees Like To See in Their Managers

Most employees receive periodic performance appraisals from managers, but managers receive little feedback on what their employees expect of them. Here are some responses to a survey from persons in the metals industry about what they expect from their bosses. Employees appreciate a manager with these qualities:

- **Honesty.** Being frank, direct, and not overselling what the manager can do for the employee.

- **Respects employees.** Most employees want supervisors to let them do the job for which they were hired. They want to be treated as adults, get assistance when they need it, and support when they are right. They appreciate a supervisor who takes time to explain new processes or changes in the work setting and who does not play favorites. They want acknowledgment that family and personal issues may at times overflow into the workplace and cause a distraction from continuing good performance on the job.

- **Listens respectfully.** Employees in the survey said they appreciate a manager who listens attentively to what they are saying, considers both sides of an issue, and then gives a decision that matches company policies or legal requirements.

- **Says "Thank You."** Workers want good work acknowledged and appreciation shown. Complimenting an employee at the workstation, honoring them in a department meeting, or writing a short note of appreciation are inexpensive motivators. And they like a boss who doesn't feel threatened when an employee is recognized.

Those are the positive qualities that employees in the survey liked in their supervisors. They don't like supervisors who threaten or belittle the staff, show partiality, and match employees against each other. They don't like managers who neglect their staff and who do not back them when they act independently and correctly.

employee may lock the desk, then the employer has created a reasonable expectation of privacy that the desk will not be searched without first informing the employee.

Many companies prepare written employment policies outlining how and under what circumstances certain company property such as lockers, telephones, voice mail, and electronic mail may be used so that employees know whether they have a reasonable expectation of privacy.

C H A P T E R

4

IMPROVING QUALITY
OF THE WORKFORCE

When employees display performance problems, managers often say, "You can't get decent
help these days."

Don't blame everything on the workers. Improving the quality of an employer's workforce
requires carefully developed selection practices and
then, once a candidate is hired, good direction and
supervision on the job, supported by employer
policies that encourage positive conduct and high-
level performance.

The Basics: Why Do People
Look For Work?

As basic as that question may sound, there are
a host of reasons that people look for work. At the
start it's usually the need for money to gain the
basics of life—food, shelter, clothing, transportation, and the like.

Beyond the basics, people seek jobs for many reasons. It's important that managers understand these reasons, since they are factors in hiring and placing that person in a job in which everyone hopes he or she will be satisfied and successful.

Some persons are looking for just a plain job, so that money comes in each week to cover the essentials of living. If a job is not available at your company, they may go next door or down the street to apply for work. Others are seeking a job opportunity—a career—from which, with good performance, they can advance.

Others seek work anywhere that offers an easy commute. Others seek favorable working hours or part-time work arrangements to match the needs of their family or social life. Some seek evening and night shift hours.

Some try to find an easy job, one that does not try them physically or mentally. Some persons with disabilities seek jobs that match their abilities and may require accommodations by the employer that allow them to perform that job.

Some companies, in turn, hire workers as "general help" or in the "labor pool," which offers employees an introduction to the company.

Some persons, plain and simple, are just looking for a job, any job. However, an employer with professional selection standards will soon find that not every applicant is a match for jobs in that company.

Finding and Keeping Quality

The first step to finding, hiring, and keeping the best workers is to assess the present situation: competition for workers in the local labor market, the business plan for the company, and the expected competition for new people in the local area, or, on a regional or national basis, for professionals and managers.

Hiring the right people is impossible unless you know who and what you want. If the job and the desired qualifications are defined poorly, it may be difficult to attract—and retain—the type of person needed for effective performance in the organization.

A successful hiring strategy includes effective interviewing techniques, forms, and processes that draw out information about the candidate, and, once the person has been hired, continuous activities to motivate that person to superior performance.

The task of screening applicants legally without violating the privacy and constitutional rights of prospective employees is not always easy. Therefore, developing company procedures for evaluating new hires should be coordinated by an experienced human resources professional, with a maximum of line and staff managerial input. The final plan should then be reviewed by a labor attorney so that the new program meets requirements of federal and state laws.

Techniques to Improve the Quality of Your Workforce

Using professional personnel management techniques will help enhance the quality of person joining the workforce. These selection procedures can be handled by line managers in small companies, but are more likely to be successful when handled by an experienced human resources professional.

These are not brilliant new or magic ideas, but rather the careful working of selection techniques, which allow an employer to focus on the best candidates for a given job opening.

Improving the quality of applicants doesn't happen automatically. Improving selection techniques takes time; expenditures for telephone calls, correspondence, and reference checking; and, for upper level managers and professionals, background investigations. Employers unwilling to assign staff to do this work will limit the quality of applicants hired.

Managers may have feelings about what makes the "best" candidate for a particular job opening; but remember: to avoid lawsuits and discrimination charges, the safest approach is to insist that all qualifications or job-required characteristics are job-related.

A carefully planned and executed selection process will eventually reduce hiring costs and turnover, result in shorter training cycles for new employees, and improve productivity sooner. Finding the "right" new hires will have a positive effect on the organization and result in better interaction of all employees.

Here are some time-honored techniques to improve the quality of the selection process:

Employment application forms.   As unusual as it may sound, some companies still hire new employees without knowing their work background or education. These people do not complete a company application form and sign only forms required by the government, such as a W-4 tax form and other legally required items. These employers know very little about their new hires and whether they will fit in the organization; if they don't fit, these new hires are dismissed quickly.

29

At the office and professional level, candidates who submit resumes to a company should also be asked to complete the employer's employment application form. That form should raise questions that a resume does not provide, since a resume is designed to present the applicant in his or her most favorable light.

A good application form should request detailed information about the applicant's qualifications and work experience as they relate to the particular employment needs of the business before an interview takes place. Signing the authorization section of the application will remind the applicant that falsification of information is grounds for termination. Employers should require that each question or section of the application form be completed and that the applicant sign the form acknowledging that they have provided all information requested.

Getting at the truth of an applicant's education and work experience presents challenges for hiring managers. Interviewers should focus on gaps in the employment history. If a criminal conviction (rather than an arrest) is shown on the application form, interviewers may ask for details. A criminal conviction need not be a bar to employment for every job. The challenge is to verify job-related information about an applicant so that a fair evaluation may be made of all candidates and a job offer made to the most qualified applicant. The problem is that some applicants make untruthful statements about themselves or show work experience or education that never occurred. In most organizations, lying on an employment application form or making material omissions is grounds for termination.

Reference checks and background investigation. Verifying an applicant's background takes time, effort, and determination to get the full story on a person's background. Doing that verification work is imperative for some sensitive or public service jobs because the employer could later face a charge of negligent hiring if the checking is not done carefully and the efforts to verify information are not well documented.

The importance of checking a candidate's references or investigating and documenting the person's work record and qualifications cannot be overemphasized. Employers have a right and a need to know whom they are hiring.

Checking references is made more difficult with the reluctance of many companies to give out information about former employees because of the risks of defamation law suits. Many companies limit the

Checklist for References

Checking references can be time-consuming but is a necessary part of the candidate evaluation process. Here are suggestions:

❏ Check out verifiable facts and statistics with the candidate's former employer. Ask for names of former supervisors, and street address and telephone numbers of these former employers. This thoroughness will leave an impression with the applicant that the employer is serious about checking references. Do not mark comments on the employment application itself, but keep a separate record showing the information received or information the prospective employer was not able to confirm.

❏ Personnel offices of former employers are not likely to know much detail of the employee's work performance, so the personnel representative may want to try to talk to former supervisors. If this is possible, ask the former supervisor questions only about job-related matters and work attitudes that affected performance.

❏ For higher level candidates, background checking may include driving and criminal records, academic credentials, and business references. Professional investigation agencies can handle this type of work for the employer and ensure accuracy. If a credit reporting agency is used, the applicant should be advised in advance.

❏ If driving a company vehicle or a personal vehicle on company business is part of the job, get a copy of the applicant's driving record, which is available through many states' department of motor vehicles for a small fee.

❏ If you encounter discrepancies between what the candidate reveals and what you learn, ask for his or her side of the story. Some people can explain job gaps or other incomplete information on an application form.

If background checks or other procedures reveal lies or conflicting information that the new hire submitted, management should review the situation immediately and where cause is established, terminate the employee.

information they will release to the dates of employment and positions held—and little more. Requiring an applicant to execute a signed release can prompt a former employer to release more than just the basics.

Some states recognize legal actions for negligent hiring when an employer fails to investigate work, education, and personal statements to see if the person poses an unacceptable level of risk. Employment representatives must be thorough and document their findings to resist any claim of negligent hiring.

Employers generally enjoy a qualified privilege when they divulge job-related information to a person with a business reason to know. Legislation in an increasing number of states now protects employers who give good faith reference information to prospective employers.

Progressive managers know the importance of investigating job applicants and taking careful and methodical approaches to reference checking that help the employer's defense against any discrimination or legal claim.

If candidates provide information on the application and resume that cannot be checked, the employer may want to bypass that applicant.

Train interviewers. Job interviewers and line managers must avoid a minefield of possible discriminatory questions and judgments. Interviewers must also ask questions and interpret responses in ways that identify individual aptitudes and attitudes that best match the needs of the organization.

Experts in the field remind us of these maxims:

- Develop specific job descriptions and requirements and use these to form a check list of questions that the interviewer asks all applicants.

- Most interviewers talk too much about themselves and their company.

Too often interviewers are busy making the applicant feel at ease (important in its own right!) or talking about their own career. Don't forget the purpose of an interview: to assess the applicant's qualifications as a possible match for the job opening. A good interviewer should be listening 80% of the time to the applicant's responses and reactions.

- Remember that the best predictor of future performance is past performance. Ask the candidate what he or she has done. An

 32

applicant with patterns of past achievement is likely to succeed in the future.

■ Who should conduct the interview? The personnel representative may conduct initial screening but certainly the immediate manager should make the final decision. Some companies insist that two managers do the interviewing, since one manager may pick up signals missed by the other and a two-manager process reduces the likelihood of biases on the part of one interviewer.

Present realistic job previews. One of the reasons for high turnover in some organizations is that too little attention is given to telling—and showing—the job for which the applicant is being considered. It's a good practice to explain details of the job, but it is even better to take the employee to the work site and show the job in operation.

An applicant for a sheet metal job may be asked to cut and form sections of sheet metal. A word-processing operator may be asked to type a sample document. These kinds of job-oriented tests are effective and permitted under the ADA.

Providing realistic job previews will reduce dissatisfaction and turnover. The recruiting department can assist in this role, but even more important is the department supervisor, who can show how the job is carried out and assess the applicant's response.

Insist on substance abuse screening of final applicants. More employers are screening applicants for illegal drug use as a condition for employment. Several federal laws specifically require preemployment drug testing of new hires—for example, the federal Department of Transportation requires such testing for long distance truck drivers—and the ADA allows an employer to conduct preemployment substance abuse tests at any stage of recruitment. The ADA does not protect active drug abusers, but protects rehabilitated drug users or those who were incorrectly designated as such from discrimination.

Some state laws also permit or require employers to conduct drug and alcohol testing in specific situations, but some state laws protect active substance abusers.

Consider skill and personality testing of applicants. Employers are often tempted to initiate testing procedures for new hires. Proponents of job testing say that testing can predict the candidate's work behaviors and chance of success on the job. However, job test results

33

should not dictate hiring decisions. Testing should be used as one tool in the selection process—in addition to the application form, interviews, references, medical examinations, and any other considerations.

Tests should be avoided unless test scores and job performance are closely correlated. Employers should monitor scores; if groups that traditionally have suffered from discrimination are shown to fail in significant numbers, the employer must validate the test by using a government-dictated mathematical formula that measures the extent of the disparate impact.

Honesty and integrity tests are professionally developed psychological tests designed to determine the integrity of test takers by measuring attitudes toward theft and propensity for stealing. These tests are favored by employers whose employees handle money or merchandise.

The Employee Polygraph Protection Act of 1988 prohibits the use of polygraph tests by private employers in most circumstances. Under certain conditions, employees suspected of workplace incidents resulting in economic loss—such as theft, embezzlement, sabotage, or injury to the employer's business—may be required to submit to a polygraph test. Employers are required to post a notice outlining employee rights and highlights of the Act.

Managers who are considering using skills or psychological tests should be fully aware of government requirements on employee testing at the federal and state level. In hiring a test supplier, determine how long the organization has been in business and ask for copies of their validation studies for the tests you are considering.

Require employment medical examinations. Many companies require that new hires have medical examinations before they start work so that they are not exposed to workplace conditions that would cause or aggravate a health problem for themselves or co-workers.

Provisions in the ADA govern the conduct of employment medical examinations and return-to-work medical examinations following an illness or work injury. The ADA generally provides that:

- Medical examinations of new employees may be conducted only after a job offer has been made. They must be mandatory for all employees, disabled or not, for the particular work classification.

- Any medical examinations required by an employer following the absence of an employee for illness or injury must be job-related.

■ Inquiries about medical conditions before a job offer is made are prohibited, and only questions about the ability of the applicant to perform a specific, job-related task are permitted.

Once a conditional job offer has been made, employers may ask disability-related questions, provided they are asked or required of all employees in the same job category.

Some states have even more restrictive provisions for employee protection than the federal ADA. These rules should be reviewed so that the employer is in compliance with both federal and state requirements.

Assess a policy on employment of relatives.   When a good employee refers a relative or friend for a job, many employers want to think that the recommended applicant will automatically fit the job or company. This is particularly the case in small businesses, which are magnets for family members and friends of employees.

The major risk in employee referrals of family and friends is that good feelings may replace good judgment when qualifications are reviewed against the specific needs of the job. That's why many companies are concerned about nepotism—the employment of relatives in the same organization. On the positive side, employers who permit such relationships believe that they provide a family-like and close working atmosphere in the workplace.

But nepotism without controls can lower workplace morale if family issues get mixed up with business matters. Other workers may perceive that family members get hired without qualifications or get favored treatment on the job.

Screening procedures for a family or friends' referral should be the same as for all candidates. References should be checked as carefully as for any other applicant.

Nepotism is not prohibited under federal law (charges of discrimination could be filed under Title VII). Many state and local human rights laws prohibit discrimination based on marital status. Some states prohibit the use of antinepotism policies (California, for example). Those few companies whose policies prohibit employees' spouses from working in the same company have sometimes been faced with gender discrimination suits, unless the employer can show a business necessity for the rule.

Employers have a legitimate business interest in regulating relationships between supervisory personnel and employees to avoid conflicts of interest. Restricting such relationships may be necessary to avoid the appearance of favoritism in the workplace. Any policy developed to limit nepotism should emphasize that the business does hire qualified relatives of employees, as long as the company retains the right to determine whether a conflict or potential conflict exists.

Require probationary periods.   Many organizations require employees to work a probationary or introductory period of time before being considered a regular employee. (Note the designation "regular" rather than a "permanent" employee—which could imply that the person has the job forever.) Sometimes probationary increases are implemented with satisfactory completion of the probationary period.

If a company decides to have a probationary period for new hires, the following should be considered in the procedure:

- No federal law governs probationary periods; review state laws to see if there are restrictions.

- Be sure the company's application form has an employment-at-will statement that allows the employer—and the employee—to terminate the work relationship at any time.

- Provide for a written review of work performance at least once during the probationary period.

- Decide on probationary periods that tie in with the complexity of the job, say 45 days for general factory work, and perhaps up to one year for managerial or complex technical jobs.

Use job descriptions.   Job descriptions are the starting point in developing a wage structure that determines the relative worth of each job to the organization so that salary or wage grades can be assigned to a job. Moreover, good job descriptions will assist staff in recruiting, hiring, and placing employees according to their skills and physical abilities.

Written job descriptions outline job responsibilities and duties with factors such as training and experience required for the job, responsibility for operations, mental and physical skill required, and working conditions.

Although no government law requires employers to develop job descriptions, the ADA says that persons with disabilities may be required to perform the "essential" function of a job, with or without reasonable accommodation, but candidates could not be required to perform the lesser or "marginal" functions of the job as a basis for disqualification in the selection process. The ADA says that written job descriptions, prepared before recruiting begins, can help the employer substantiate the requirements of a job.

Implement "Standards of Conduct."   Some companies call them plant rules; others label them standards of conduct or guidelines for behavior. No matter what they're called, these lists of do's and don'ts on the job are what the employer expects in the way of personal conduct at work and, in some cases, what the penalties will be for misbehavior. This is another method of communicating performance requirements to employees.

Some companies do not believe in these types of regulations, reasoning that adult persons know what is right and wrong in the way of conduct at work. These organizations prefer to retain a broad license to discipline as needed.

Work rules typically list guidelines for attendance and punctuality and eating and smoking areas and prohibit soliciting on company property, consuming alcohol and drugs on company premises and using company telephones, and the like. Plant rules should be reviewed at least annually or, when changes in company policy, procedures, or federal or state laws occur.

Remember, these suggestions when developing standards of conduct for the workplace:

- The tone of work rules should be positive and upbeat, placing responsibility on the employee to use common sense and good judgment in conduct at work.

- Each rule should be reviewed to make sure that it does not violate a federal or state discrimination law. Work rules must be able to stand up to the scrutiny of government investigators, who may be investigating a discrimination charge by a present or former employee. These compliance officers will ask if the employer has company rules, whether they are posted and publicized widely, and how management has applied discipline in similar cases.

- The employer should retain the right to establish reasonable rules to regulate and control employee conduct. Wording about discipline and penalties should be general, such as ". . . including, but not limited to the following. . . ." so that management

37

retains broad powers to analyze each case and apply discipline appropriate to the circumstances.

Progressive discipline is generally regarded as a positive employee relations approach, but employers should not get trapped into a policy of progressive discipline for every offense. In a serious incident, the employer may want to suspend the employee while the matter is investigated. If the facts warrant it, it may be appropriate to convert the suspension to a termination.

- For a unionized workforce, plant rules are one of the conditions of employment. While work rule changes should be communicated to the union and their input invited, management should not require the union's approval of the rules.

Require performance evaluations. Many line managers view the task of completing a performance evaluation on their employees as a laborious annual job, part of a routine that has something vaguely to do with the amount of an annual increase or merit adjustment for the employee. In many organizations that is indeed the only function of a performance evaluation.

An annual performance evaluation should be a summary of the employee's work that the supervisor has already commented on— positively or negatively—during the course of the evaluation period. It should not be a surprise to the employee.

Managers should be trained in performance management and how to complete the performance appraisal form objectively and fairly. The system must gain credibility with employees by rewarding higher levels of performance with higher levels of merit increases.

Performance appraisals must be specific enough to motivate good, poor, and mediocre performers, but they must be based on specific job requirements (as shown in an up-to-date job description), defined goals and performance against those goals. Vague or generous appraisals without specifics can come back to haunt an organization that wants to terminate a worker for unacceptable performance.

An honest critique of an employee's work is essential if the employee is to have fair warning of the need for improvement. Attitudes on the job that affect job performance should be discussed. The performance review discussion should give the employee time to air concerns, ask for advancement or transfer, and discuss obstacles he or she encounters in performing the job. Good performance should be confirmed formally in the evaluation.

Insist on effective orientation procedures. New hires should undergo an orientation procedure that will provide them with basic information about the job and the company. The meeting should make them feel that they have selected a company that is interested in its employees.

Orientation should include completing the necessary company employment forms, including verification of eligibility to work in the United States (the I-9 form). Company information documents, including an employee handbook, should be provided. Company policies on harassment should be covered in this session and the organization chart with names and numbers should be explained so the new hire will know where to go with questions or concerns.

Company safety and security rules and general information on company benefits should also be covered, although some companies prefer to get into this type of detail in a formal orientation several weeks after the employee starts work.

The new employee should be turned over to the supervisor for department introductions, familiarization with the department and work area, and job training. In some companies, a job instructor or mentor is appointed to guide the person through the first few months on the job. The department supervisor or job instructor should review job or department safety rules.

These general orientation procedures should be adapted to the company, department, and job assignment, depending on whether the employee is a managerial professional, office, plant, sales, or technical hire. A well-planned orientation process for new hires may take time to plan and organize, but it makes for a positive introduction to the company.

QUALITIES OF SUCCESSFUL APPLICANTS

What qualities do productive members of the workforce share? There are some common denominators that can be checked to see if the hiring manager leans toward the applicant most likely to succeed. Managers should decide if the applicant has:

- An educational and/or work background—the knowledge, skills, and abilities—that parallel closely the job specifications. A written job description listing essential functions of the position helps the recruiter and reminds the hiring manager that these indeed are the job duties.

- Career ambitions for which the opening is the next logical step; or, in the case of a lateral move, a job transfer that will provide new experiences at the same level of responsibility.

- Employment or has been laid off for legitimate business reasons.

- A stable work record, consistent work history and job responsibilities, and no unexplainable gaps in the resume.

- A salary history and objective that fits into the salary range of hire.

- Willingness to work in the community and can readily commute by personal or public transportation to the job.

- An attitude that supports a positive work ethic.

Not every final applicant fits neatly into this desired list, but using these types of guidelines should reduce the candidate list to those who are most likely to be successful.

TRAINING YOUR EMPLOYEES FOR NEW OPPORTUNITIES

Many U.S. companies have their eye on today—keeping production high, the plant efficient, and their customers satisfied. Too few are interested in investing in their employees' future—which is the company's future—by offering training and development opportunities within the organization.

Training employees in new duties is an investment in tomorrow and a positive indication that the organization offers more than a job to the employee—it can offer a career.

In today's information economy, the pace of change and technological advancement is so intense that we all need to be lifetime students. To stay competitive in the global economy, we must keep updating our education and training through our entire working lives. Progressive employers visualize this concept and offer in-company or inservice training and refresher courses to their employees.

Pay and Benefits

One of the principal ways to retain good employees is to offer competitive rates of pay and medical and insurance benefits. Very good performers will need to be paid above the norm, through salary, incentives, or bonuses. Uncompetitive salaries, wages, and benefits are one of the triggers that start employees looking for another employer and "a better job."

Provide awards and rewards. Good performance should be acknowledged prominently and employees rewarded in either monetary or nonmonetary ways. Positive reinforcement ensures the continuation of good work.

A good merit increase or a one-time bonus that honors good performance is one of the most direct ways to reward employees. Gaining favor these days are alternate monetary rewards—year-end incentive payments or even one-time awards of shares of company stock. These are direct rewards and make an impression. Monetary awards should be made promptly, as soon as possible after the significant event.

Nonmonetary awards can be equally impressive and can make an even bigger impression on an employee. A commendation directly to the employee while working, a letter of appreciation directed to the employee's home, or a compliment paid to the employee in a crew get-together or a business meeting all leave their positive mark on the employee and the work group.

Pictures of employees in a company publication or special honors at a company function can work wonders for morale. Some organizations present plaques or other visible awards for employee achievements.

Whatever method is used, rewards and awards can enhance the work of good employees and encourage their continued employment with the organization.

NECESSARY PROCEDURES FOR DISCIPLINE

Even with great care in hiring, a few "problem employees" are likely to find their way onto the payroll. In every organization a small percentage of employees do not perform to expectations and must be corrected so that the work of good performers is not dragged down and morale and efficiency lowered.

Many employers subscribe to the principle of progressive discipline, unless the facts of the case warrant immediate suspension or termination. In most organizations, progressive means counseling or a verbal warning to the employee on the first offense; repeat offenses are followed by written warnings, a disciplinary suspension, and finally, termination. The range of penalties before termination depends on the organization's view of discipline and severity of the incident.

Once company policies are established and communicated to employees, managers and supervisors must be trained to administer the policies fairly. A key role of a manager is a willingness and ability to confront employees with performance problems and take appropriate corrective action. Careful, documented discipline is the best way to improve the employee's performance and decrease the employer's exposure to discrimination and wrongful discharge claims. All this presumes the existence of accurate personnel records.

Legal Guidance

Competent human resource managers can provide the day-to-day guidance at the work site that line managers need to conduct their dealings with employees and do it legally. However, some situations may require the help of another professional—the employment law attorney.

An employment law attorney should be consulted when an employee's rights may be at question—for example, if management plans to search an employee's locker or if a long-term employee will be accused of stealing. Legal services are used infrequently, but they should be sought to guide management in the correct handling of special situations.

 42

PART

II

PROBLEMS ON THE JOB

CHAPTER

MANAGING PERFORMANCE PROBLEMS ON THE JOB

The front-line supervisor is the person who manages an employee with performance problems. Supervisors know the people who work for them, are familiar with their work record, work habits, conduct, and appearance on the job. Monitoring employee performance that is crucial to the success of an improvement program is an integral and accepted part of a supervisor's job.

Any worker may experience difficulties in work performance at one time or another, but it is when these problems interfere with continued good job performance that the person becomes a "problem employee." Next to the employee with the performance problem, the supervisor has the most to gain from effective management of the employee.

Managers face many types of performance problems. How well supervisors can handle these problems, turning unsatisfactory performance into more acceptable performance, is a hallmark of their success at workplace leadership.

Performance problems can stem from marriage and family, finances, physical and mental health, job stresses, co-workers, and other supervisors and managers. Substance abuse—including addiction to alcohol, prescription drugs, or over-the-counter medications—is an increasing factor in the deterioration of job performance.

How an employer approaches performance problems will influence the manager's actions in correcting errant work behavior. A few organizations offer limited or no corrective efforts and quickly terminate the employee with declining performance; other companies engage in progressive discipline efforts as the best road to correction.

Throughout this process, managers need to be mindful of the federal, state, and local laws that govern the employment relationship. The human resources professional should be up-to-date on these regulations and provide training and guidance on company disciplinary procedures and applicable laws.

Correcting Performance Problems

Management's view of correction and the organization's culture will fashion and flavor the corporate approach to correcting performance problems. If the employer believes in the progressive approach to performance improvement, then the period allowed for correction should not be open-ended—that is, progress should be reviewed at appropriate intervals—say, 30, 60, or 90 days—so that improvement or regression is formally monitored. Specific objectives and measurements of progress should be established and committed to writing. The agreement should provide that if reasonable progress toward the goal is not evident, the employee can be demoted or terminated at any time. But whatever approach is taken, a central ingredient must be the employee's commitment to improve.

No Single Answer

There is no single, magic wand that can solve all problems with employee performance on the job. There may not be one right answer for two workers with the same problem. The facts, causes, and reasons of each situation must be analyzed so that a performance improvement plan can be developed.

The immediate supervisor has the responsibility to monitor variances from normal performance, gathering initial information on the deviation or performance problem, investigating if need be, speaking to the employee, and trying to develop improvements in performance. The manager may not have to do this alone and should reach for line and staff assistance if and when needed. Higher levels of supervision or management can assist, as well as specialists from the human resources or personnel management function.

Supervisors may have opinions as to the causes of declining performance, but they should remember that they are not health care professionals. Often highly specialized training is required to make an accurate diagnosis of the true cause of an employee's health or physical problem.

Here are some practical guidelines for a supervisor in approaching a performance problem.

Recognize the unique role of a manager. Managers have a unique place in the lives of their employees, who look to them for leadership and example. Supervisors who help and encourage their employees to do their job productively and safely contribute to the employee's sense of security, self-respect, confidence, and identity. Many are authority figures, since they have the power to say "yes" or "no" to employee requests or make recommendations concerning their wages and conditions of employment.

Supervisors have legitimate concerns for total job performance which they, as part of management, have every right to expect. Managers who ignore or attempt to cover up performance problems do their employees a disservice.

Try to identify the symptoms. When a performance problem develops, supervisors should try to identify the symptoms of the changed behavior on the job—slower or faster pace than normal, disregard for quality, quietness or liveliness, fear, anger, inattention to work, increases in absenteeism, disputes with co-workers, or unsafe work behavior. Each supervisor should be alert for what detracts from normal or standard performance, since monitoring job performance is a key supervisory responsibility.

Document performance variances. All persons, including managers, exhibit performance problems occasionally. Supervisors should document patterns of declining performance over time, as part of their responsibility for monitoring an employee's performance and conduct in the work environment.

The facts of the employee's performance that do not meet established, minimum standards should be observable and measurable—fewer production units on the last shift, poor quality on Order X, removing safety guards when operating machinery on Line # 2, etc.—not subjective opinions. Documentation should state what a person did or said or facts about their appearance or work habits that affected performance.

Document each occurrence of a problem immediately. Don't wait until later, and don't describe problems generally. The record should be dated and signed by the supervisor recording the incident. Inadequate documentation is a principal reason why supervisors are often unable to justify their disciplinary decisions.

Review performance variances with the employee. Supervisors should discuss substandard behavior or declining performance with the employee. Violation of important company rules is serious misbehavior on the first incident; other performance problems become serious when repeated.

Before meeting with the employee, the supervisor should know clearly what is to be discussed—objective facts or information that affect job performance. In the course of the conversation, the supervisor tries to get agreement that there is a performance problem.

Ask the employee for input on what needs to be done to return performance to satisfactory levels. Reach agreement with the employee on what specifically will be done to correct the problem.

Listen a lot. Psychologists say that listening is probably the single most effective technique for helping people with problems, including work performance problems. Listening allows the employee to vent—to get the problem off his or her chest—clarify thoughts and feelings, and reduce tension. At appropriate times the supervisor should restate and clarify—ask questions if the employee's words are not clear. Use open-ended questions so the employee has to respond at length rather than provide "yes" or "no" answers. Summarize at the end of the discussion— it reassures the employee that the supervisor has indeed been listening. As the last item in the session, set a date for a follow-up discussion.

If improvement is evident, encourage and support it. If in the follow-up session the problem is not clearing up, discuss how the employee is not keeping his or her commitments.

Help is available. Supervisors should recognize when to refer an employee to someone else—maybe someone in the human resources department, the medical office, in an employee assistance program (EAP), or community counseling service. Be careful when making a referral, since specific referral requires a diagnosis that is beyond the supervisor's role.

The employee who does not accept this referral and whose overall work performance continues below minimum performance standards should be given a firm choice between seeking assistance or accepting the consequences of deteriorating performance—the appropriate disciplinary action set by the organization.

COMMON CONCERNS: FACT SHEETS ON GENERAL PERFORMANCE ISSUES

In the following section we will discuss general performance issues and offer you avenues of solution for you to tailor to your specific needs. Each section includes a description of the nature of the problem, important issues to consider, any applicable government regulations, suggested action steps, and a listing of resources to assist in your resolution of the problem.

ABSENTEEISM

Nature of the problem: Employers can reasonably expect employees to come to work regularly and to report to work on time. Absence and lateness are problems that often confront line managers early in their job assignment. Tardiness is a form of absence and is covered in another fact sheet.

Patterns of absenteeism vary and can include Monday and Friday absences, repeated absences and—the key—a higher absence rate than other employees. It is a gnawing problem that befuddles many supervisors.

Seasoned managers have heard all the excuses—the flu, the car wouldn't start, the babysitter has quit. Although most excuses are legitimate, none of them help the manager get the job done.

Many of the things that keep people from coming to work are beyond the supervisor's control. That's why the manager should focus on the problems with job performance that absences cause—transferring another employee to cover the job, the work does not get done for the day, the need to call in another employee, etc.

Several federal government laws and some state laws provide for approved absences for certain specific conditions (see "Applicable Government Regulations").

Many companies recognize that some employee absences will occur and allow for a number of paid sick days or personal days each year. Many organizations have set up no fault absentee policies or "leave banks," which allow employees a prescribed number of days of absence each year for any reason—valid or otherwise. After that predetermined number of days has been used up, discipline triggers quickly, and termination soon follows. Other companies take a strict view of the problem—employees are expected to be in regular attendance, period.

Still other organizations have found it necessary to establish absence control programs to remedy the problems or, failing that, to discipline and terminate repeated offenders.

A key ingredient of an attendance control policy is accurate documentation—that is, a listing of absences and the stated reasons for those absences, compared to other workers or the "average" incidence for the facility. Personnel departments are often asked to coordinate the documentation of absences and the reason for the absences. Generalizations do not make much headway here; specific facts must be used to confront the employee.

Issues to consider: Managers should consider the following issues when assessing performance problems caused by absences:

■ Does the organization have an established, publicized policy on regular attendance and what will be done to those who are unable or unwilling to meet the policy requirements?

■ Is a formal reporting system in place to document absences?

■ Do managers follow up on absences to be sure that the person is fit for work on the next working day? Do managers insist that the employee call directly to the manager to report an intended absence?

■ Is regular attendance listed as an "essential job function"? For example, a line mechanic may be needed every day if this person's work supports the work of the assembly line crew, and production may be stopped when the mechanic does not show up.

■ Is progressive discipline used to bring the matter of absences forcibly to the attention of the errant employee? Is discipline applied uniformly and without discrimination?

■ Are mitigating factors involved in any of the absences?

■ Are the absences the result of job injuries or illnesses or non-occupational factors? Job-related absences are usually easier to document. Is medical documentation required for absences beyond a given number of days?

■ Are persons who are bored with the job or don't feel appreciated using sickness as an excuse to stay away from work?

■ How does the employee's absence rate compare with the average rate of absences in the facility or nationwide? (See Resources to Assist) The following formula can be used to develop absence rates:

$$\frac{\text{\# of worker-days lost through absences during the month}}{\text{average \# employees} \times \text{\# of workdays in the month}} \times 100$$

ABSENTEEISM

■ Does a state law affect an employer's absence recordkeeping? Some state laws, for example, require exclusion of any work-injury absences from a benchmark absence control program.

Applicable government regulations: The federal Family and Medical Leave Act (FMLA) permits some absences from work. Eligible employees are entitled to up to a total of 12 weeks leave without pay during any 12-month period for the birth of a child, placement of a child for adoption or foster care, an employee's serious health condition, or caring for a spouse, child, or parent with a serious health condition.

Action steps: Managers should consider the following when developing a policy to control absences:

■ Employers should have written attendance guidelines that incorporate applicable provisions of the federal Family and Medical Leave Act. The policy should also outline steps managers should take when employees do not meet the prescribed guidelines. Employees need to see that the supervisor and the company are serious about absences.

■ Be sure the employer's attendance guidelines are publicized and well communicated to employees.

■ Managers should insist that calls reporting absences come directly to them or an immediate assistant. The manager should ask what the problem is and how long the employee expects to be away from work, and express the hope they will get well quickly. If the manager's comments are sincere, people will miss fewer days.

■ Does the company policy require medical documentation for both job-related and nonoccupational absences?

■ Watch for patterns of absences. Off-the-job social events or perhaps a recurring duty on the job may cause the employee to avoid those duties and stay away from work.

■ Absenteeism is often listed as an area for the application of progressive discipline. Employers should apply discipline in a uniform manner for similar types of offenses. Be sure that any absences are not protected absences under the FMLA. Check, too, on any provisions of the ADA that may apply.

■ Welcome back each person who's been absent. Tell the worker that you are glad to see him or her back, ask how he or she is feeling, and listen if the employee wants to tell you about being sick. Listening shows you care.

Resources to assist: The Bureau of National Affairs (BNA) publishes a quarterly report on job absences and turnover. The more than 300 companies surveyed are divided into manufacturing, nonmanufacturing, and nonbusiness organizations. The survey shows incidence of absences by region (northeast, south, north central, and west) and by number of employees ranging from fewer than 250 workers to 2,500 and more. Information is available from BNA, 1-800-452-7773.

Some state business and industry associations and chambers of commerce keep similar statistics.

ABSENTEEISM

ACCIDENT REPEATERS

Nature of the problem: Injuries incurred by "accident prone" employees, including on-the-job accidents, frequent trips for first aid or medical treatment, off-the-job accidents that affect job performance, unsafe work habits, and violation of safety rules, exceed those of other employees who do similar jobs.

A variety of health, psychological, and physiological reasons can contribute to the problem of one employee having more accidents, on average, than other employees. Fatigue and stress can preoccupy a person so that full attention is not devoted to the job. Drugs and alcohol dull reaction times. Individuals with disabilities such as impaired vision or hearing may be more susceptible to injury. Young, untrained, workers may take chances on the job, resulting in a higher number of accidents. Older workers may have injuries as the result of diminished hearing, slower reaction times, or inattention due to overfamiliarity with the job. Split shifts or night shifts can tire workers and reduce a person's reaction times, resulting in more accidents. Some industries—electrical, chemical, nuclear, construction, and mining, among others—present hazards above the norm. However, sometimes workers are involved in accidents frequently because they disregard basic safety rules.

Industry statistics are not available to measure the number or percentages of workers who are considered to be accident-prone. It is certain, though, that in every facility in America some employees have more accidents than "average," which can be measured by reviewing the first aid log, the OSHA Log of Recordable Injuries, and workers' compensation reports of injuries or job illnesses.

Issues to consider: It's easy to jump to conclusions about accident repeaters. It's better to try to identify the problem so that corrective action, based on facts, can be taken. Managers should consider:

- Reviewing company first aid logs and the OSHA 200 Log for several years to focus on any individuals who repeatedly suffer injuries. Is it the individual or the job that causes the injuries? From these logs, plantwide or department averages can be generated so that the individual's record can be compared to these averages.

■ If an employee is trying to exceed productivity norms to earn a higher incentive or bonus. Is the employee working too quickly? Is he or she a well-intentioned worker who gets hurt because—like Superman—the employee thinks he or she has unlimited physical powers?

■ Off-the-job pressures that may be affecting the person's attention on the job, or is the individual's health deteriorating, thus affecting job performance? If so, is an employee assistance program in place to help the employee? Are long hours or heavy overtime causing fatigue that results in injuries?

■ Many organizations include in their plant rules provisions for disciplining employees who disregard safety rules. (OSHA does not have authority to discipline or fire employees who do not comply with OSHA standards or employer safety rules. It is the employer's obligation to enforce these rules).

Applicable government regulations: Several federal laws, including the ADA and OSHA have provisions that may be applicable to accident repeaters.

Under the ADA, an employer may not inquire into an applicant's workers' compensation history until after a job offer has been made, and an employer may not base an employment decision on the speculation that an applicant may cause increased workers' compensation costs in the future. However, the employer may refuse to hire or may discharge an individual who cannot perform a job without posing significant risk of substantial harm to the health and safety of the individual or others, if the risk cannot be eliminated by reasonable accommodation.

OSHA requires training of employees in the safety requirements of their jobs under many of its standards. Also, the federal Act, under its General Duty Clause (Section 5 (a) 1), requires employers to provide "employment and a place of employment which are free from recognized hazards that are causing or likely to cause death or serious physical harm. . . ."

Action steps: The manager has the key role in spotting, then correcting, unsafe work behavior. Supervisors who know their employees will be able to take note of any behavior out of the norm. Supervisors

ACCIDENT REPEATERS

need to find out why injuries are occurring through accident investigation procedures.

It's best to identify the specific problem of accident repeaters so that corrective action, based on facts, can be taken.

- Focus on the individual. Talk with the employee to review the accident history, emphasize company safety policies, and decide how unsatisfactory behavior, once known or discovered, can be changed. Solicit the worker's input and ask: "What do you think needs to be done to correct the problem?" Results of the meeting should be documented.

- The level of employee's on-the-job training should be reviewed. Is retraining necessary? Will temporary assigning of a job instructor, mentor, or trainer help correct the behavior?

- Is the problem an individual problem or is it accident repetition by a group of workers doing the same job? That should lead the manager to investigate what's wrong with the job—inherent hazards—with the employees who do the work.

- Is a transfer to a less demanding job in order? Some people cannot adapt to machine-paced operations, yet perform well as "solo" operators or in service jobs.

- Some employers include accident repeaters in safety activities such as a safety committee. Such involvement sometimes generates increased interest and corrects the problem. Be careful that an accident repeater does not drag down the positive efforts of other safety committee members.

- Employers should be prepared to take action against employees who have repeated, preventable accidents, since these injuries and incidents are legitimate performance issues that should be addressed through the corrective action process.

- When appropriate efforts have been made to correct the situation and these have failed, management action is needed. The organization cannot permit repeated unsafe acts that result in harm to the employee, co-workers, or company property to continue. The company policy on discipline and termination should govern further steps to take.

AIDS AND HIV INFECTIONS

Nature of the problem: AIDS is a viral condition that impairs the body's ability to fight infection and makes patients susceptible to rare and opportunistic diseases. The difference between a person with AIDS and a person who is HIV positive is determined by whether the individual has contracted certain infections and/or has sufficiently impaired blood cell counts.

HIV infection and AIDS are chronic illnesses that can result in declining work performance.

HIV cannot be contracted through ordinary workplace contacts. HIV is spread by exchanging body fluids—by sexual contact, sharing a needle with an HIV-infected person, during pregnancy, or passed by a mother to a baby when nursing. More than one million persons are estimated to be infected with HIV in the United States. Although new drugs offer hope for many people, prolonging and improving their quality of life, there is no cure for AIDS at this time, and most people ultimately die of the disease.

Issues to consider: When analyzing a job performance problem that may be caused by a person who has AIDS, managers should consider:

- To what degree is the person's illness affecting job performance? An HIV-infected person can remain productive for 10 years or more. As the HIV infection progresses into AIDS, the illness may prevent an employee from performing regular jobs or being in attendance for full-time employment.

- If job performance declines, are there vacant jobs or other jobs to which the person can be transferred and perform productively?

Applicable government regulations: The ADA lists AIDS and HIV infections as covered disabilities under the federal disability protection law. Company policy should state that the organization does not discriminate based on disability of chronic illness. Be sure that company medical policies do not discriminate against persons with terminal illnesses.

Federal OSHA's Blood Borne Pathogens standard provides control procedures for first aid and health care industry workers who are called upon to treat illness, injuries, and wounds and may have exposure to body fluids.

Action steps: Supervisors should consider these accommodations when managing an employee who has advised the employer of AIDS or an HIV-infection:

- Persons needing to attend doctors' appointments can benefit from a flexible work schedule that allows them to attend medical appointments during working hours.

- If job performance declines, to which vacant or alternate jobs can the person be transferred and perform productively?

- In those workplaces such as hospitals and correctional institutions where there is potential risk of exposure to blood, employers should provide training and appropriate personal protective equipment to ensure that infection control procedures are followed.

Resources to assist: National Leadership Coalition on AIDS, 1400 I Street, Washington, D.C. 20005 (202 408-4848. Offers managerial educational materials on HIV infections and AIDS.

ALCOHOLISM

Nature of the problem: Alcohol is a depressant that can impair the person's judgment, coordination, retention, and memory reflexes. A person under the influence of alcohol may not be able to operate a motor vehicle or machinery safely. Alcoholics may present excess absenteeism, lateness, or lengthened lunch periods, restlessness, erratic behavior, and mood swings. Chronic alcohol dependency can result in medical conditions such as liver damage, hepatitis, altered brain cell functioning, gastritis, and impotence.

About 10 million persons in the United States are classified as alcoholics. It is estimated that five percent of employees in any industry have a drinking problem. More than 40% of all traffic fatalities involve persons under the influence of alcohol or other drugs.

Issues to consider: Alcoholism is a personal health condition and the confidentiality of medical information is protected under specific provisions in the ADA. Managers are not physicians and should not diagnose health conditions, including possible alcoholism.

Managers who suspect an alcohol problem with a worker should consider the work performance aspects of the problem:

- How is job performance affected by the suspected alcohol problem? Are there deteriorating problems such as absences from work, lowered productivity, poor quality, or inability to communicate with managers and co-workers?

- Has the employee disclosed to the manager that he or she has a drinking problem?

- Does the immediate supervisor or the employee's co-worker cover up for the alcoholic employee by doing the employee's work?

- Does the company have a formal policy prohibiting the use of alcohol on the job or on company premises?

- Does the employee have access to an employee assistance program (EAP) through the company or in the community?

ALCOHOLISM

Applicable government regulations: The ADA considers alcoholism to be a disability. Employers are prohibited from discriminating against employees solely because of diagnosed alcoholism, unless they pose a direct threat to the safety and health of themselves or other workers in the department. Persons with alcohol related conditions can be held to the same performance standards as other workers.

Action steps: Supervisors should consider the following steps when managing an employee with a suspected alcohol problem:

- Focus on the performance problem—what on the job is not going right. To repeat: Managers are not physicians and should not act as either doctors or diagnosticians. The emphasis should be on work performance and the deterioration that is caused by a problem.

  Managers should be concerned with the individual's job performance. The diagnosis of the ailment should be left to professional health care providers. Supervisors should insist that production, quality, and safety standards be met by all employees.

- If the employee has admitted to an alcohol problem, then employee commitment is the key to recovery. The motivation to recover must be with the employee and continue with the employee through recovery. Organizations such as Alcoholics Anonymous and any local employee assistance program can help.

- If early recovery efforts are unsuccessful, the employee should be offered a firm choice between improving job performance or undergoing treatment. If that does not work, then the company's policy on formal disciplinary action should be invoked.

Resources to assist: National Council of Alcoholism and Drug Dependence, Inc., 12 West 21 St., New York, NY 10010. (800) NCA-CALL, provides education, information, help, and hope in the fight against the chronic and often fatal disease of alcoholism and other drug addictions. Many of NCADD's affiliates provide employee assistance programs or referrals and intervention services.

Alcoholics Anonymous has many local contacts throughout the country. Check the local telephone directory. The General Services Office of AA is at 459 Riverside Drive, Box 459, Grand Central Station, New York, NY 10163. Telephone (212) 870-3400.

ANGER

Nature of the problem: Everyone has feelings of anger from time to time that are not violent or considered out of control, but uncontrolled anger is a powerful force that can intimidate others and make them upset. Anger can give the angry person great physical power and may result in violence.

Anger often develops when an employee feels that someone is treating them unfairly, that another person is taking advantage of them or they feel the impending threat of some kind of loss.

An angry person can disrupt the workplace and lower morale. Productivity and safety can be affected. In a severe form, anger borders on violence in the workplace.

For the angry person, the emotion can lead to severe mental and physical conditions, including depression, heart attack, and stroke.

The angry worker is difficult to manage, and getting the person to perform assigned duties may, in the minds of some managers, be more trouble than it is worth. But because of potentially disruptive effects by the angry person, that approach should never be taken. The problem should be faced.

Issues to consider: Anger that is allowed to continue unmanaged can evolve into a long, drawn-out series of destructive thoughts and actions. One employee's anger can breed retribution responses in other employees. In assessing this problem, managers should consider:

- What can the employee do about controlling anger? If the employee knows that controlling anger is a problem, he or she may realize that a "time out" for themselves—a chance to walk away from the worksite for a few minutes to cool off—is necessary.

- What is the effect of the anger on co-workers? If it is a single incident and quickly over, it is usually soon forgotten. If anger persists and involves damage to products or equipment or an attempt at physical harm to a manger or other employees, it must be handled immediately.

- Has the employer included in the plant rules a ban on weapons at the workplace and promoted a weapons-free environment?

Applicable government regulations: There is no federal regulation on anger in the workplace, but OSHA, under its General Duty Clause (section 5 (a) 1), requires employers to provide "employment and a place of employment which is free from recognized hazards that are causing or likely to cause death or serious physical harm to his employees. . . ."

Action steps: Managers who encounter chronic anger should first make a major effort to "keep their cool" before talking to the upset worker. Then they should consider these steps:

- What has provoked the anger? Sit the employee down privately and allow the person to vent his or her feelings. Be patient. Allow enough time so that the angry person expresses everything. The manager should listen, acknowledge, and not interrupt.

- What can be done to modify the employee's thoughts and actions? Listening to the person's concerns should allow the manager to focus on the emotions and the reason for them. Focus on the negative emotions and try to find out what can be done to turn them around into energy-producing, positive efforts. Such a step involves the employee's understanding of what causes the anger and a commitment to change his or her ways.

- How can anger be managed in the future? After the manager has found out what's wrong and, it is hoped, corrected the problem, then he or she should have a basic idea how to forestall out-bursts in the future. What does the employee suggest to correct the problem? If the employee understands what is wrong and what to do to correct the wrong, then the employee is more likely to control excess emotion. Encourage positive behaviors and review and help the worker focus on the causes of the nega-tive behaviors and the commitment that was made to correct those behaviors.

- Alleviations of chronic anger may require referral to a health care professional, an employee assistance program, or community health agency.

- Serious incidents of anger at the worksite should be treated as an incidence of potential violence and the matter should be addressed immediately, including removal from the job or assis-tance from security personnel or police in removing the em-ployee from the workplace.

ATTITUDE PROBLEMS

Nature of the problem: "Poor attitude" is a subjective assessment of a person's outlook and is often difficult to document, but negative employee attitudes can translate into trouble on the job and create performance problems and harm morale among other employees.

Attitude problems can result from poor health, family problems, money stresses, or poor motivation towards the job and company.

The key point: Is there a performance problem as a result of the personality trait or attitude? A person who is indifferent and has negative attitudes may perform well on the job and not have a harmful effect on the productivity of other workers.

Managers should be concerned when unsatisfactory attitudes start to affect the employee's work performance or that of co-workers.

Issues to consider: Employees are entitled to have feelings and attitudes about a host of things that affect them on the job. A manager should be concerned about only those attitudes that affect job performance. Managers who feel an employee has an attitude problem should investigate further and ask:

■ Are the employee's attitudes affecting their own work performance or the productivity or quality of the work of other employees? That should be the determining factor—its effect on job performance.

■ Is the unsatisfactory attitude caused by the company's culture or the job?

■ Are employees asked for their opinions and input on plans and decisions affecting them? Involvement tends to generate enthusiasm and interest in activities, including job activities.

■ When attitude problems overflow and become a work performance problem, do employees know about company rules and are they forewarned of the consequences of violating them?

ATTITUDE PROBLEMS

ATTITUDE PROBLEMS

Action steps: Managers should avoid the term "attitude" when discussing the performance problem with the employee. Call it unsatisfactory behavior or conduct.

- Managers should not focus on the attitude itself but what the attitude causes the employee to do—or not do—on the job. Be specific. Describe how the behavior affects work flow or job performance and the negative effect it has on the ability of the department to achieve its goals. Show how the behavior affects other employees in the work unit.

- Once the negative consequences of the action have been explained and the necessity for positive conduct is outlined, the responsibility for correction shifts to the employee. What suggestions does the employee have to correct work behavior that is affecting the work performance of the unit?

- If a counseling or disciplinary action is necessary, be prepared to focus on specific results that the unsatisfactory demeanor caused. The focus should be on job-related behaviors and standards.

- Document counseling or other personnel action. That documentation may relate to a violation of company rules, low production performance, unsatisfactory quality caused by the employee behavior on the job. Be sure that any intended corrective action is similar for related cases and is not discriminatory.

- Develop a performance improvement plan, ideally incorporating the employee's own suggestions.

CHRONIC COMPLAINERS

Nature of the problem: Employees' outlook about work and life in general can affect their work performance. Attitudes that result in complaining may have deep roots, and discovering the reason and doing something about it isn't always easy.

Every organization has chronic complainers. For these people, little is good and most everything is bad or wrong. They look for problems with the job, managers, co-workers, and the work environment. They will find reason to complain about anything—supervisors, work methods, fellow workers, product quality requirements, food in the cafeteria, overtime requests, and parking spaces in the parking lot. These people can quickly become "a pain" to fellow workers and try the patience of a supervisor.

The complaining may arise from work-generated problems (not enough supplies, too much work, poor coordination with another department) or may be the result of friction between personalities (off-the-job personality conflicts, poor communication skills, smokers vs. nonsmokers).

Anti-authoritarian types may challenge the manager's responsibility in telling them what to do; indifferent employees may resist when the supervisor tries to upgrade their efforts. These attitudes don't always exhibit themselves directly but may result in other signs—absenteeism, poor job performance, or poor relationships with co-workers.

Supervising a chronic complainer is not an easy task. Supervisors who do this well say they focus completely on work performance, disregarding the complainer's commentary. Some supervisors with serious cases of chronic complaining have had to take disciplinary and even termination action when they found that these persons detracted from efficiency in the department and lowered the morale of co-workers.

Issues to consider: Managers trying to develop corrective action plans for the chronic complainer should consider these issues:

- What is bothering the complainer? Pay close attention to what the employee says or does and to the circumstances that accompany the negative behavior. Ask the employee directly or listen to

65

other managers who may have insights into the reasons for the problem.

■ Does the employee have a legitimate complaint? Justifiable complaints should be investigated and avenues of resolution discussed with the complaining employee.

If the complaining is unfounded and it continues detracting from the employee's work efficiency or that of co-workers, then counseling and disciplinary action should be taken. A bad apple can't be allowed to sour the rest of the good apples.

Applicable government regulations: Federal and state safety standards allow employees to complain about legitimate safety concerns on the job. Such complaints should be investigated promptly and corrected where cause is found. If the investigation finds no valid basis exists for the complaint, then communicate that result to the employee.

Employees have a right to complain about what they feel is discriminatory treatment in regard to wages, hours, and working conditions on the job. Such protection is built into federal laws such as the ADA, Title VII, and other statutes.

Action steps: Each person who is considered a moaner or groaner needs to be assessed individually and differently. Through all the words and complaints try to:

■ Meet with the employee privately. Listen; don't argue with the employee or push your own point of view. Don't agree with the employee, but rather, make the employee feel that you take what he or she has to say seriously.

■ Understand the causes for the dissatisfaction. Give the employee your attention and ask open-ended questions to encourage the employee to talk. Often employees need to vent, to get something off their chest.

■ Find any element of truth in the employee's story and address those, even when the employee's attitude is unreasonable and exasperating. Ask for the employee's input by saying: "How would you solve this situation?"

■ Emphasize that you want to be on the employee's side. Often this will help them to think more positively. Say you want to work with the employee, and mean it. If that offer to help is followed up and reemphasized, a change of behavior might occur.

■ If it turns out that the attitude is only in the employee's mind, the problems may be solved in a series of meetings, giving the employee time to reflect between meetings.

Good communication skills can help you. Openness between you and your employees is essential to minimize negative dispositions.

DRUG ABUSE

Nature of the problem: Drug abuse is the consumption of substances to the extent that normal life functions and judgment are impaired.

Drug use can alter behavior, mood, and attitude. Physical symptoms can be acute, including loss of motor skills, hyperactivity, and hallucination. Many substances lend themselves to abuse. Alcohol is the most widely abused substance. Glue, paint thinner, over-the-counter diet drugs, and even animal tranquilizers are common drugs of choice. Many people become addicted to prescription drugs such as Valium or codeine. Millions of Americans use marijuana and millions use cocaine.

Issues to consider: The employer should consider that some drug use might occur at the worksite.

- Does the employee exhibit unsteady gait, slurred speech, or argumentative behavior? If so, it may be a wiser first step for the manager to label the conduct as "unsafe work behavior" or "reporting to work under the influence" until additional information can be obtained.

- Does the employer require substance screens for prospective new hires? Such a program, carefully established and administered, will go a long way to filter out active substance abusers before they get on the payroll.

- Does the employer have antidrug abuse policies and procedures to help employees? Availability of an employee assistance program will help.

- Is the employer in an industry with safety-sensitive jobs where postaccident drug testing is appropriate and legal? Federal and state statutes on postaccident drug testing should be checked out.

Applicable government regulations: The ADA does not protect active drug abusers but does offer protection to persons who are participating in a supervised drug rehabilitation program or have completed such a program and are no longer engaged in illegal drug use. Also protected under ADA are those persons who are perceived to be drug users, but are not.

Some state laws are more conservative and restrict premployment screening for drugs, random testing, and postaccident testing.

Action steps: The core of an employer's policy should encourage strong job performance and, when a deterioration in performance is observed, confrontation and a disciplinary process should be initiated. Steps to take include:

■ Develop antidrug abuse policies and procedures, communicate them to employees, and enforce them.

■ Develop comprehensive drug education information. Prepare training materials for supervisors on how to manage the suspected drug abuser and materials for employees and their families.

■ Require drug screening of new hires. Depending on the industry and any applicable government laws, conduct random screening for substance abuse among those holding safety-sensitive jobs.

■ Offer the services of an employee assistance program (EAP) so persons with this problem can take advantage of a rehabilitation program.

Resources to assist: Drug-Free Workplace Hotline, sponsored by the National Institute for Drug Abuse. 1-800-843-4971. Helps employers with materials to develop a drug-free workplace program.

DRUG ABUSE

FAMILY PROBLEMS/WORKLIFE ISSUES

FAMILY PROBLEMS/WORKLIFE ISSUES

Nature of the problem: Family problems or worklife issues can weigh heavily on the mind of an employee, causing distractions, loss of productivity, inattention to quality, and accidents. A serious health condition or the care of a close family member may require time away from work, as provided by the FMLA for eligible employees.

The Act promotes family-friendly policies to assist the affected employee including part-time work schedules, flexible work time scheduling, intermittent leave, and job sharing. Certain highly paid key employees are exempted from coverage under the Act.

A human resources professional is an excellent resource for managers who need guidance in administering FMLA. It is important to train managers in details of the law, company policies implementing the law, and how to handle individual requests for leave. Labor department or company forms should be available so employees may formally apply for the leave. The employer or manager must then respond to the request in a timely manner, preferably in writing.

The employee is protected under the Act from any adverse action or retaliation as a direct result of taking FMLA leave, regardless of how disruptive such a leave may be to the employer's operations. The well-prepared manager should be able to plan for these eventualities in the same manner as other operational interruptions.

Managers should seek guidance before taking any disciplinary action against an employee for absences, since intermittent illness/absences may be protected under the Act.

Issues to consider: Managers who face a request for time off from work by an employee for these worklife issues should consider the following factors:

- Is the employee eligible for the leave?

- Is the request covered under provisions of the FMLA or its state equivalent?

- Are notices and postings required under FMLA posted on notice boards?

■ Does the employer have a written, publicized policy covering leaves of absence for family needs? Is there a conflict between federal and state requirements? Remember, the conditions that benefit the employee most take precedence.

■ What strategies are in place to cross train workers to cover other jobs during periods of vacation, personal illness, or family leave? Consider such approaches as job rotation, apprenticeship programs, internships, job sharing, and flexible scheduling. Can some duties be reassigned to other employees? Can the present skills of employees be enhanced with additional training? Could employees from a temporary agency cover the absence?

■ Do you have a long-term strategic plan for employee development?

■ At performance review time give employees a goal: Develop your own replacement within the year!

Applicable government regulations: The FMLA permits employees with certain specific family situations to have up to 12 weeks' leave without pay in a 12-month period. The Act applies to employers with 50 or more employees regularly employed within a 75 mile range, except that the 50-person threshold does not apply to public sector employees or to public or private schools. To be eligible for the leave, employees must have been employed for at least 12 months and worked at least 1,250 hours of work during the 12-month period before the leave.

Medical benefits in effect before the leave must be continued on the same basis during the leave. At the end of the leave the employee must be able to return to the same position or a job with equivalent pay or benefits.

Employees requesting leave must give the employer 30 days' notice, or as soon as practicable, under the facts and circumstances of the situation. Written notice cannot be required in the case of the employee or a family member's serious health condition. The employer may request medical certification of the need for a leave. Good documentation of the reason for the leave is an absolute essential.

Some state laws provide benefits that exceed provisions of the federal law. Managers should check with their human resources department to determine exact provisions.

An employee who feels that benefits of the family and medical leave act have been denied may file a discrimination charge with the Equal Employment Opportunity Commission.

FAMILY PROBLEMS/WORKLIFE ISSUES

Action steps: To administer requests for leave and the federal FMLA, managers need:

- A company policy on how requests for family leave will be handled, including provisions of the FMLA, and the forms to request a leave.

- Supervisors need to be trained in the provisions of the law and applicable company procedures. Provisions should be included in the employee handbook, if such a document is used.

- Managers should survey their departments to determine needs for cross training workers to cover other jobs during periods of vacation, illness, or family leave. Can present skills of employees be enhanced with additional training to cover the absence? Will it be necessary to hire other employees—perhaps from a temporary agency—to cover the absence?

- Establish a neutral leave policy, in accordance with provisions of the FMLA and the ADA. Requiring the termination of an employee after all leave entitlements have been exhausted is often prescribed, if the employee has not returned to work. But managers are cautioned that each situation should be reviewed on a case-by-case basis.

INSUBORDINATION

Nature of the problem: Insubordination in the workplace is the refusal of an employee to comply with the direct order of a manager to perform a job-related duty. It is failure to submit to the employer's right and authority to run the business, challenging the manager's delegated right to direct the operations or service functions.

The traditional approach in the manager-worker relationship is for the employee to "obey now and grieve later," except when certain situations arise, such as:

- Obeying the supervisor's order would result in a life-threatening or serious injury situation to employees

- Following the supervisor's directive is clearly against the law or public policy

- The act is discriminatory

Issues to consider: Managers facing insubordinate work behavior by an employee should consider these issues:

- Is the order clearly a job duty, in conformance with company policy and the law?

- What is the damage, if any—work left undone, products reworked, safety and health dangers, extra scrap generated, customers angry? While insubordination is not condoned, the extent of the damage of the insubordinate behavior should be considered.

- Does the employee know how to perform the duty, or has the employee been trained to perform the work safely? Is protective equipment necessary for performance of the duty readily available?

- Has the employee clearly heard the directive, understood the order, and knows what is expected? Remember that some employees have hearing impairments, may be distracted, or may not hear clearly if the order is given in a noisy environment. Ask the employee specifically if the order is understood. Some managers go the extra step to restate the order in a quiet environment and in the presence of another supervisor. In the case of a unionized location, have a union steward present.

- Have the consequences of failure to obey the order—discipline or termination—been outlined to the employee? Does the employee understand and acknowledge the consequences of failure to obey?

Supervisors should be wary of taking any action before they have all the facts. Depending on company policy and the seriousness of the incident, they may want to review the matter with upper management or a human resources professional. Once the supervisor has investigated the facts, a course of disciplinary action, assuming discipline is warranted, should be decided on. While most rule infractions require progressive discipline, some serious misconduct may merit immediate termination.

Applicable government regulations: Managers should have a general knowledge of government regulations that may affect the giving of orders—the National Labor Relations Act, the FMLA, the ADA, the OSHA.

Action steps: An outright refusal to perform a normal job duty can be considered insubordination, which is then subject to discipline, suspension from work, and/or termination.

Managers faced with this type of situation should:

- Assess whether the employee understands the order and the consequences of not carrying out the order. Check to make sure that the employee understands what you want—a basic feedback theory.

- Determine whether the employee has adequate training and/or experience to carry out the job duty.

- Take time to cool off, if either the employee or manager have gotten angry and lost objectivity in the matter.

- Repeat the directive to the employee in quiet, private surroundings, away from other employees, and in the presence of another supervisor.

- Give the worker the opportunity to return to the work station and carry out the order and not hover over the employee.

■ Ask the employee to sit in an office or conference room and the manager, if necessary, should obtain additional advice from superiors or a human resource manager. The manager may choose to ask, "Why are you not carrying out this direct order?" Listen with an open mind. Then, depending on company policy, the employee may be suspended or terminated, depending on the seriousness of the infraction, the employee's work record, and the handling of similar situations in the past.

■ Exercise care to select the particular rule that most appropriately applies to the alleged offense. Instead of insubordination, it may be more appropriate to label the misconduct as "failure to operate power press in conformance with company operating instructions" or "refusal to wear respirator in confined work space, per company safety rules."

INSUBORDINATION

75

LEGAL DRUGS

Nature of the problem: Employers are properly concerned about the use of illegal drugs in the workplace, but there is another concern that can affect productivity and employee performance: the use of prescribed and perfectly legal drugs which may also affect job performance and employee and co-worker safety.

The most commonly used prescription drugs include sedatives, sleeping pills and anti-anxiety medication. For the majority of employees the use of prescribed and perfectly legal drugs for personal health conditions is temporary; and for most there is no problem continuing with their regular work. But an employee who is prescribed legal drugs by a health care provider can develop side effects which affect the employee's productivity and safety on the job.

Some of these legal drugs can slow a person's reaction time, impair memory and body motor coordination which can be particularly frightening in a work situation where co-workers may be depending on that person to react quickly in a work safety situation.

Older persons taking prescribed medications can face slower reaction times and this makes for double jeopardy in a work setting where key employees are usually longer service—and older—employees.

A very small percentage of persons on regular medication become addicted to prescription drugs. A few even shop physicians asking to continue prescriptions that will keep their habit going.

Issues to consider: Supervisors are not physicians and should not attempt to diagnose the problem. If the supervisor spots drowsiness on the job, the employee should be questioned in an effort to determine the problem. In those locations with a medical department, trained medical personnel should be asked to assist.

Applicable government regulations: The ADA requires, among other provisions, that an employee's medical information be kept in confidential files, separate from personnel files, and be released only to safety and other personnel only if there is a concern about safety of the employee or co-workers.

Action steps: Employees themselves who are taking prescription medications with possible side effects can take steps to prevent this problem on the job. They should acquaint their physician with the nature of their work and any safety implications, before prescription drugs are ordered. The health care provider should then advise the employer about any restriction in work assignments that should take place while using these drugs. The employee should also abide by any warning labels affixed to prescription bottles.

Managers should consider these alternatives when assessing the possible effects of legal drugs on the job:

■ Don't ask employees about prescription drug usage unless the manager has a legitimate, business-related reason for doing so.

■ A temporary reassignment away from machinery, for example, may be appropriate until the employee finishes use of the medication and can return to a regular job.

■ Persons taking addictive, legal drugs can be a particular problem as they often do not realize they have a problem. Family members can often help in confronting a loved one and insisting that they get help. A medical examination may be appropriate. Encouraging such an employee to take advantage of Employee Assistance Program (EAP) services is a positive step.

LEGAL DRUGS

LITERACY

Nature of the problem: Depending on what study you review, the illiteracy rate in the United States ranges from 10–50 percent of the population. The federal Department of Education says that some 27 million adults read at or below the fourth grade level and are regarded as functionally illiterate.

These statistics are scary when they are related to the employer's need to have persons who can read job and safety instructions. For employers the problem can be translated into those who do not read at all, those people who do not read as well as others but generally get by, and those who read well and can understand job manuals, equipment notices, safety signs, raw material and chemical cautions, labels, and instructions.

Few employees are willing to admit they can't read or write well, or that they have trouble understanding English. Some pretend they are not interested in the material when they are really trying to avoid having to read what is in front of them. The social conditioning of some employees also may discourage them from asking of questions.

Issues to consider: Managers who encounter a reading problem among workers should consider:

- Experts say that a low level of literacy skills does not necessarily mean a lack of intelligence or job skills.

- Is job performance satisfactory? Many persons with reading and comprehension problems find informal ways to overcome their deficiencies.

- Will individual tutoring or mentoring help? Perhaps a friendly supervisor or a well-regarded job instructor can offer the needed remedial training informally to overcome the specific problem.

- Can community literacy programs or an employer-provided program assist? Basic skills training should be part of a total training package to minimize any embarrassment to persons with low reading skills.

LITERACY

■ Ask for volunteers to do reading; don't put persons with literacy problems on the spot to read.

Action steps: Employers who find a significant reading comprehension problem should consider:

■ Examine training materials to be sure that they are written at a worker reading level, rather than a college reading level.

■ Include literacy training in a low-key way as part of a total training activity with learning materials directly related to workplace goals. Frequent feedback, related to the goals of the training activity should be provided

■ Design training materials which rely less on reading. Written text can be supplemented with graphics, videos. A picture is *still* worth a thousand words.

■ Tie text to real-life, on-the-job occurrences to emphasize problems or successes.

Resources to assist: *The Right to Understand: Linking Literacy to Health and Safety Training* by Elizabeth Szudy and Michelle Gonzalez Arroyo, Labor Occupational Health Program, University of California Regents, 2514 Channing Way, Berkeley, California 94720.

LITERACY

79

MEETING PRODUCTION REQUIREMENTS

Nature of the problem: Some jobs such as service jobs do not require an employee to meet specific production figures. Where specific productivity levels are required, however, the inability of a worker to meet production requirements is usually quickly noticed and becomes an immediate performance problem for the supervising manager.

When employees are unable to meet production requirements, the question raised immediately is: What are the production requirements? Jobs that have been surveyed in time and motion studies by a person such as an industrial engineer can have specific requirements (to produce x units per minute or per hour, allowing for fatigue, rest time, and the like) applied to them.

It is difficult to discipline an employee for inability to meet production requirements when these are vague numbers, often subjectively developed by a supervisor or set at the level of the "best" producer. Jobs that are paid on incentive quickly show who can meet production requirements and who cannot, since some or all of the pay is based on the number of quality units produced.

Issues to consider: Management should consider these factors when assessing low productivity:

■ Has a standard of production performance been determined and is it reasonable? Is individual performance measured against this standard?

■ Has the standard of performance been communicated clearly to employees? Do they know what is expected of them and have they been trained on how best to achieve the production requirement?

■ Can low productivity be attributed to other factors, such as an unusually high volume of business, problems with raw materials or equipment, or other untrained workers?

■ Are there extenuating circumstances—is the job too much for one person or are there conflicts within the crew?

80

■ Was the employee trained on the job? How long has the person been performing the job, compared to the average time for good production on the job?

■ If there are measured production requirements, what is fair output for the employee, considering job experience and factors such as fatigue?

Applicable government regulations: The Civil Rights Act of 1964 and its amendments prohibits discrimination in compensation, terms, and conditions of employment because of race, religion, color, sex, or national origin.

The Equal Pay Act of 1963 prohibits paying workers of one sex less than the rate received by those of the opposite sex for jobs substantially similar or identical in skill, effort, and responsibility performed under similar work conditions.

Action steps: A manager faced with a problem of low productivity should inquire:

■ How has the employer handled these types of incidents in the past? Is there a company policy or procedure that will help guide a manager to improving low productivity?

■ Are the production standards reasonable, and have the standards been communicated to the employee? If not, be sure to do it.

■ Using those standards as a gauge, does the employee in fact have a low level of productivity? Is it the lowest level of productivity in the work unit?

■ Is the employee at fault for the low productivity, or are other factors such as machine performance, inadequate training, or quality of materials involved?

If satisfactory answers are not provided to the above questions, then it is possible that the person may not be a good match for the employer's needs. Counseling, transfer, discipline or termination may be appropriate, depending on the company's policies and procedures in such areas.

MEETING PRODUCTION REQUIREMENTS

MEETING QUALITY STANDARDS

Nature of the problem: There is no single, correct definition of quality. Some would define it as "conforming to specifications" or "meeting customer needs"; others would say it is "zero defects," and still others define it as meeting a particular company quality standard for the particular production run involved. The correct answer is the one that produces the results sought by the manufacturer or provider of a service and its customers.

The organization that improves quality reduces the amount of rework and scrap involved, cuts inefficiency, and raises productivity. Good quality improves customer satisfaction and improves the company's bottom line.

Failure to meet quality standards is a principal reason that many workers fail on the job. It is exceeded only by poor productivity as a source of unacceptable employee performance.

There are four key features in successful quality management— sufficient training to perform the job, understanding what the quality specifications are, giving employees the time and equipment to produce a quality product or service, and rewards for achieving good quality work.

Issues to consider: Managers trying to solve a quality problem should consider:

■ Are quality standards specifically defined, or is a verbal okay from the supervisor acceptable?

■ Have customers defined the level of quality they want in the product, or is it left to some vague, subjective determination? Customers don't always state their requirements as specifically as they might, but it's their judgment of the work—whether to accept or reject—that counts. Reaching agreement with the customer in advance eliminates the surprise of nonconforming outputs.

■ Are quality checks made at each step of the production process so that further damage is not done to the product? Are errors caught and corrected as quickly as possible? When specifications

MEETING QUALITY STANDARDS

are specific and clear, a set of measures can be attached to each step of the work process to determine whether the task is being accomplished within established parameters.

- Who is responsible for quality—the person producing the product or providing the service, or the quality control department? Quality cannot be inspected or built into a product after the fact by the quality control department. The quality control department audits the level of quality; production mechanics and operators are the employees who produce a quality product or service at each stage of the process.

- Are workers trained in specific quality requirements of the product or service, and are samples of acceptable and unacceptable quality available as a guide?

- Is equipment maintained and serviced regularly so that it can produce an acceptable, quality product?

- Do managers provide positive feedback to employees who produce quality work—and counsel and redirect those who don't?

- Have arrangements been made to rework rejected materials or products so that they can be made into acceptable levels of quality?

- Are the numbers of quality errors measured so that feedback can be provided to managers and workers?

Applicable government regulations: The Civil Rights Act of 1964 and its amendments prohibits discrimination in compensation, terms, and conditions of employment because of race, religion, color, sex, or national origin.

The Equal Pay Act of 1963 prohibits paying workers of one sex less than the rate received by those of the opposite sex for jobs substantially similar or identical in skill, effort, and responsibility performed under similar work conditions.

Action steps: Managers need to understand the importance of quality leadership and goals and the role in achieving a competitive advantage. In turn, they must champion specific quality standards, encouraging those who met the standards and investigating human, machine, or material error when satisfactory quality is not produced.

MEETING QUALITY STANDARDS

In solving a quality performance problem, managers should ask:

■ Is the individual employee adequately trained so that he or she feels responsible for producing a quality product?

■ Is quality assessment and reporting structure in place so that managers and employees receive prompt feedback on their work performance? This is best accomplished by an audit process that tracks variances from specifications.

■ If quality variances exist, is an investigation held to determine the cause? Is corrective action implemented? If training of new workers or retraining of experienced workers is needed, the needs should be handled through training activities that attack the problem areas.

■ Continuing good quality performance is a precious thing and the basis of a company's success. Managers need to compliment those who produce quality work and confront those who don't by involving themselves in retraining, counseling, and discipline, if necessary.

MENTAL ILLNESS/DEPRESSION

Nature of the problem: The fear of being stigmatized because of a mental illness has caused many people to hide their conditions from employers. Although most cases of mental illness are caused by factors unrelated to work, some job-related situations can trigger depression or worsen an existing mental health condition. Mental illnesses are not the result of personal weaknesses or bad upbringing.

The National Institute of Mental Health estimates that 22% of all adults will experience a diagnosed mental illness in their lifetime, roughly one out of five persons. One in 20 workers is believed to suffer from some sort of clinical depression.

With psychotherapy and/or medication, most mental illnesses such as depression can be successfully treated or controlled.

Issues to consider: Persons with mental illness may have difficulty in screening out noise and other distractions, maintaining concentrations for long periods of time, meeting deadline pressures, and responding to change.

Persons with depression often have three types of work-related problems:

- High absenteeism

- Difficulty in completing work assignments

- Fear of making presentations to others

The work-related problems often make it difficult for managers to distinguish people with mental illness from employees who are just poor performers. On the other hand, many people with mental illnesses are excellent employees and satisfactory work performers. Mental illness does not always interfere with a person's ability to work successfully.

Mental illnesses should be diagnosed by a professional—and a manager should not guess at what causes the employee's problem. Substance abuse is sometimes a secondary problem to mental illness.

But the employer need not tolerate serious workplace disruptions or violence merely because the employee has a mental illness.

MENTAL ILLNESS/DEPRESSION

Applicable government regulations: The ADA considers mental illness and depression as "covered" disabilities under its provision, and employers are prohibited from discriminating against such persons because of their disability. The persons, of course, must be able to perform the essential functions of the job.

Not all mental illnesses would qualify for coverage under the ADA, since they do not "substantially limit one or more major life activities" of the individual, and most people with mental conditions do work.

The employer should focus on the qualifications of individuals for the particular job and whether an appropriate accommodation will enable the person to perform the job. The requirement that employers provide reasonable accommodation for people with covered mental disabilities means that employers may have to put up with minor inconveniences or disruptions that do not rise to the level of preventing others from performing their jobs.

Action steps: Here are some suggestions for managers faced with a problem of an employee with a possible mental illness:

- The best option for handling what appears to be depression is to refer the worker to the facility medical department or to an employee assistance program. Supervisors should confront an employee and let them know that there is a work-related problem and that something needs to be done. Supervisors have to be careful but assertive when trying to persuade an employee to seek help.

- Some type of accommodation may help the person with a mental illness—a self-paced workload or a flexible work schedule that allows the person longer lunch and break times, job modifications that could include transferring marginal duties of the job to other workers, or a temporary accommodation to a fixed shift rather than working rotating shifts. Some persons with mental disorders are allowed to work at home. Two or more persons may share a single job.

- In some cases, written job instructions may lessen distractions on the job; modifying the work area to minimize distractions can also help.

- If reasonable accommodations are required, consult with the employee for suggestions on what might help.

■ Myths and stereotypes about people with mental illnesses may make some employers concerned about on-the-job safety. It may be helpful to provide sensitivity training for co-workers to develop support and acceptance of their fellow workers with mental disorders. The side effects of medication may prohibit some patients from working with heavy machinery but the effect will vary from individual to individual. Guidance should be obtained from the attending health care professional.

Resources to assist: National Mental Health Association, 1021 Prince St., Alexandria, Virginia 22314; 1-800-969-6642.

MENTAL ILLNESS/DEPRESSION

OLDER WORKERS

Nature of the problem: Workers ages 40 and over are the largest percentage of the American workforce today.

The problem of performance among older workers is usually the decline in personal capacities of persons as they get older. Sometimes—hearing, sight, reflex actions, stamina, and physical strength start to decline. These declines can affect productivity, quality, and even safety for the older employee and co-workers.

However, studies have shown that older workers are less prone to accidents than younger persons, and that learning ability, intelligence, and motivation do not decline with age. Older workers take fewer days off for illness than younger persons and bring maturity, experience, and good judgment to the job scene.

Younger managers must be prepared to handle the occasional awkwardness associated with supervising older workers. The worst scenario is doing nothing and allowing a work performance situation to deteriorate further. Younger supervisors should recognize that older worker's social and work experiences are different from theirs and respect those differences. Each person has something unique to contribute to the workplace.

Issues to consider: Managers encountering a problem with an older worker should analyze the reasons for the problem and try to get at the cause. In many cases the causes are easy to address—an eye examination may reveal a solution for declining sight, work efforts can be redirected, jobs or equipment can be modified.

Applicable government regulations: The federal Age Discrimination in Employment Act (ADEA) protects persons age 40 and over from discrimination on the job because of age. Some state laws protect persons of any age from discrimination in employment.

Action steps: Experts offer these suggestions that can help make older workers continuing contributors to the company's success:

■ Older workers tend to rely on ways that worked well for them in the past. This is usually good thinking, but new work procedures may dictate the need for supervisory follow-up on the job, redirection, or retraining.

■ Good workplace lighting will help all workers perform the job and minimize the danger of trips or falls, a common hazard for older persons.

■ A manager who feels that an older worker has a performance problem should speak to that employee without referring to age. Try to develop a performance improvement plan. Friendly guidance and redirection can go a long way to help an older worker adapt to new directions at work.

■ Use the best qualities in older workers. Top-performing older workers can be asked to help as trainers and mentors of younger workers.

Resources to assist: The Worker Equity Department at the American Association of Retired Persons (AARP), 1909 K Street, N.W., Washington, D.C. 20049 offers pamphlets including a booklet *"How To Manage Older Workers"* and training materials to help employers assimilate older workers in the workforce.

OLDER WORKERS

PERSONAL HEALTH CONDITIONS

PERSONAL HEALTH CONDITIONS

Nature of the problem: Personal health problems can quickly result in a decline in employee work performance. Some personal health problems may be chronic, including conditions such as diabetes, high blood pressure, migraine headaches, epilepsy, or emphysema. Signs of physical distress include nausea, headaches, dizziness, slurred speech, disorientation, or stomach problems.

Issues to consider: Managers trying to cope with an employee's health problem that is affecting work performance should consider the following issues:

- Does the employee need medical attention? Supervisors may suggest that the employee seek medical evaluation and treatment, but remember: managers should not attempt to be physicians.

- Does the employer have a sick leave plan or disability benefit for poor health? If the employer does offer paid sick leave, the worker can be reassured that income will not stop during illness.

- Does the employer have an employee assistance program (EAP) or is there access to a community medical referral service? Remember that not all employees have a family doctor. In larger facilities, an in-house medical department usually offers basic treatment for nonoccupational injuries and illness and can act as a referral service to community health care providers.

Applicable government regulations: Several federal laws protect the worker who must have time off from work due to illness. The FMLA permits eligible, sick employees to have up to 12 weeks leave of absence without pay in a 12-month period.

Managers need to remember that workers with occupational injuries and illnesses cannot be required to take "light duty" assignments rather than a leave of absence under the FMLA. Employees may be offered alternative work assignments, but employers are prohibited from requiring them to take such assignments in lieu of unpaid leave.

Some state laws provide benefits that exceed provisions of the federal law. Managers should check with their human resources department to determine exact provisions.

Action steps: Any employee who is not feeling well should seek medical assistance. A company-sponsored medical plan will relieve worries about covering the cost of medical treatment.

Managers are not medical professionals. Confirmation of an employee's health condition should come from a licensed health care provider. If there is good reason to question the provider's statements, then an investigation should be conducted through the company medical department or human resources manager. Good documentation of the reason for the leave is essential.

PERSONAL HEALTH CONDITIONS

PERSONS WITH DISABILITIES

Nature of the problem: More than 47 million persons with disabilities are at work or are seeking work in America today. Many of these persons feel that they have been discriminated against in the past as many employers focused on their disability rather than their abilities. Persons with disabilities can perform many jobs, with or without reasonable accommodation.

Managers seeking guidance on how to manage persons with disabilities effectively should understand provisions of the ADA so that they can avoid discriminatory treatment of these persons.

Employers seeking qualified applicants should consider individuals with disabilities in the selection, transfer, and promotion process.

Issues to consider: Managers need to know the provisions of the ADA and understand its key definitions. (See the following section.)

Applicable government regulations: Two federal laws—the Rehabilitation Act of 1973 and the ADA of 1990 prohibit discrimination against employees because of a disability as specified in the Act, which applies to all organizations of 15 or more employees. The Rehabilitation Act applies only to government contractors—those companies that do business with the federal government.

Under the ADA, a disability is defined as a physical or mental impairment that substantially limits one or more of the major life activities of an individual who has a record of such an impairment, or is regarded as having such an impairment.

A physical or mental impairment is defined in the Act as:

- Any physiological disorder or condition, cosmetic disfigurement, or anatomical loss affecting one or more of the following body systems: neurological, musculoskeletal, special sense organs, respiratory (including speech organs) cardiovascular, reproductive, digestive, genitourinary, hemic and lymphatic, skin and endocrine, or

■ Any mental or psychological disorder such as mental retardation, organic brain syndrome, emotional or mental illness, and specific learning disabilities.

Major life activities under ADA mean functions such as caring for one's self, performing manual tasks, walking, seeing, hearing, speaking, breathing, learning, and working. ADA defines a qualified individual with a disability as an individual with a disability who satisfies the requisite skill, experience, and education requirements of the employment position, and who—with or without reasonable accommodation—can perform the essential functions of such position.

The term essential functions of the job means primary job duties that are intrinsic to the job. The EEOC, which is responsible for enforcing provisions of the Act, says it will consider the employer's judgment of what those essential functions are, as well as any written job descriptions.

The ADA does not define reasonable accommodation, but rather lists examples such as "modifying devices, services, or facilities or changing standards, criteria, practices, or procedures for the purpose of providing to a particular person with a physical or mental impairment . . . the equal opportunity to participate effectively in a particular program, activity, job, or other opportunity."

Reasonable accommodation also includes:

■ Making existing employee facilities readily accessible to and usable by individuals with disabilities

■ Job restructuring, part-time or modified work schedules, reassignment or modification of equipment or devices, appropriate adjustment or modification of examinations and training materials, providing qualified readers or interpreters, and other similar accommodations.

Action steps: Many persons with disabilities do not need special accommodations on the job or have found ways to perform the work without the need for special consideration. In most cases, an appropriate job accommodation can be made without difficulty and at little or no cost. An accommodation may be something as simple as allowing an employee with diabetes to work a flexible work schedule so that the employee can take longer rest periods or medication, or allowing the person with mobility impairments to eat a snack or lunch at his or her desk.

PERSONS WITH DISABILITIES

93

In considering persons with disabilities for employment or place-ment, managers should consider:

■ Interviewing the person in line with requirements of the ADA

■ Determining if the qualifications of a person with disabilities is a match for the requirements of the job. Can the person with the disability perform the essential functions of the job with or without accommodation?

■ If accommodations appear to be needed, what does the person with the disability suggest as an accommodation? The manager need not accept the suggestion, but it should be considered in the determination of an accommodation that will allow the person to perform the job effectively.

■ Follow up to see that the employee with the disability is per-forming effectively and that any accommodation provided is also working well.

POOR HOUSEKEEPING ON THE JOB

Nature of the problem: Good housekeeping is regarded as a neat and clean workplace. Good housekeeping on the job adds to workplace safety, a clean product, or better-provided service to customers. For employees who practice a neat and tidy work area, it's a sign that they care.

Poor housekeeping detracts from safety, quality, productivity, and morale and presents the risk of slips, falls, and fire. Most workers want an organized, safe work environment. Employees get upset when their co-workers leave the place a mess, especially in a shift environment where the next shift has to clean up the mess left by the preceding shift.

Issues to consider: A manager facing a problem with an employee who keeps the individual workplace untidy should consider:

■ What does management want in terms of housekeeping? A top management directive on neat, clean, and safe workplaces can do a lot to carry the message of good housekeeping down to lower levels in the organization. Take an unannounced walk through the facility and rate the level of cleanliness and housekeeping.

■ Do managers practice good housekeeping? Is the manager's office neat and tidy? Do managers bend over and pick up refuse on the floor and put it in the trash? Are spills cleaned up promptly?

■ Does the nature of the business lend itself to a neat and tidy workplace? A sales office has very different housekeeping conditions from the production floor or a foundry. The nature of the product or service performed will dictate to a large degree the relative ease of keeping the place neat and tidy at all times—yet, foundries and construction sites often have end-of-the-shift cleanups so that scrap, debris, and dirt are removed promptly to diminish the risk of fire and tripping hazards.

■ Is there a place for everything? Has management provided enough storage space—items such as a scrap bin near each machine to accumulate rejects, devices to remove trim from material at each stage of manufacturing, storage racks for ladders, bins for electrical tools and extension cords, lockers for employees' personal possessions?

■ Are floor surfaces clean, free of oil or grease? Are stairs clear of tripping or falling hazards?

■ Are raw materials and finished goods stacked neatly and pallets of finished goods strapped neatly and safely? Are containers provided for scrap or rework items?

■ Do employees understand their individual responsibility for tidiness of their own work station? Custodians and cleaners may be responsible for general areas such as aisles, locker rooms, and break rooms, but most companies require individual employees to keep their work station neat and orderly.

■ Is there a process or routine to report serious housekeeping incidents to management?

■ Is the eating of food allowed in the work area or restricted to the cafeteria or break rooms?

■ Are the rags used to wipe down machinery discarded into a special container? Improperly discarded cleaning rags can become a fire hazard and present dangers of tripping and slipping.

■ Are work clothes clean? Are uniforms supplied? Dirty and contaminated clothing should be placed in designated containers. Employees should wash up promptly after removing work clothes.

■ Is waste and rubbish removed from the facility on a frequent basis?

Applicable government regulations: Federal OSHA in its General Duty Clause (Section 5 (a) (1) of the Act) requires employers to keep a workplace free from recognized hazards and in its regulation (29 CFR 1910.141) requires that "all places of employment, passageways, storerooms, and service rooms should be kept clean and orderly and in a sanitary condition."

Action steps: Managers should realize that good housekeeping is everyone's responsibility. In enforcing a housekeeping improvement activity, they should consider:

POOR HOUSEKEEPING ON THE JOB

■ Management and individual managers should set a good example. If poor housekeeping conditions are observed, they should arrange to correct them promptly.

■ Every work item should have its own designated storage place, and the items should be returned to those places promptly when not in use. The old maxim "A place for everything and everything in its place" should be preached and practiced.

■ Each employee should understand that he or she is responsible for tidying his or her own work area. This basic principle should be publicized, encouraged, and enforced where necessary.

■ Train employees to report potentially unsafe conditions—the torn carpet edge, damaged stair steps, protruding objects, damaged tools, or any other conditions or equipment that could be hazardous.

POOR HOUSEKEEPING ON THE JOB

RELIGIOUS AFFILIATION NEEDS

Nature of the problem: Some employees may make requests for time off from work to observe their religion. Courts have generally held that employers must reasonably accommodate requests to observe the Sabbath or other religious days, unless the request would cause undue hardship to the business.

Some religions involve overt religious appearance or behavior at work—some of which can be accommodated; other demonstrative dress or activities may have negative business connotations or job safety implications and have to be limited.

The EEOC has suggested various voluntary means of accommodating the conflict between the company's work schedule and religious practices, such as:

- Promoting an atmosphere where substitutes and job (swaps) are favorably regarded

- Allowing voluntary substitutes and job 'swaps' among employees

- Publicizing policies of religious accommodation

- Providing a central file or bulletin board or other means for allowing flexible scheduling.

If an accommodation cannot be arranged, the company should document the offers of accommodation that were made and/or the hardship that would be immediately caused.

A seniority system in a collective bargaining agreement will typically override a requirement of religious accommodation.

In deciding if religious accommodation is required, courts have analyzed the "totality of the circumstances" and have considered such factors as:

- Length of time, frequency, and duration of the accommodation

- Availability of qualified replacements

- Cost of qualified replacements

- Reduced efficiency

- Number of employees requiring accommodations

- Volume of employers' business at the time accommodation was sought.

The failure of an employee to inform the employer of his/her religious needs may constitute a waiver of the right for reasonable accommodation.

Employees must first show that they have a *bona fide* religious belief that conflicts with an employment requirement, that they informed the employer, and that they were denied the request or disciplined for failing to comply with the company's conflicting requirement. Once the *prima facie* case has been made, the burden shifts to the company to show it could not reasonably accommodate the request.

Managers must realize that once the situation is known, they almost always must make a good faith effort to accommodate an employee's religious beliefs before a company can raise the defense of an undue hardship. The accommodation, however, need not necessarily be of the employee's choice.

Sensitivity, awareness, flexibility, and training in investigating and responding to religious discrimination claims is important, as well as an internal audit of corporate forms and policies to ensure voluntary compliance.

Issues to consider: In assessing a request for religious accommodation, managers should consider:

- The standard for showing undue hardship under religious discrimination has been relatively low. Employers do not have to violate seniority rights of workers, incur more than minimal expense, or deny shift and job preference of some employees to accommodate the religious needs of others.

- There's a delicate balance between constitutional protections for religion and federal and state employment discrimination laws. The First Amendment of the Constitution guarantees religious freedom to citizens, and two clauses of the Amendment can also have a bearing on employment-related matters. The Free Exercise Clause dictates that the government is not to interfere with religious practices; the Establishment Clause prohibits the government from aiding or favoring religion, mandating neutrality toward all religions.

    Some employers allow religious activities such as Bible reading or prayer at the work site during an employee's nonworking

99

RELIGIOUS AFFILIATION NEEDS

time as long as business activities are not disrupted. Religious observances may be conducted at the employee's own workstation or in common areas such as the canteen or break areas.

■ If employees complain that other employees' religious activities bother them, management should try to find out why the activity is bothersome and how important the observance is to the person who is doing it. Management should also explore whether the person engaging in the religious activities could make adjustments to avoid conflicts with co-workers.

Problems occur when religious observances overflow into company time and interfere with other employees' ability to do their work.

Applicable government regulations: The First Amendment of the Constitution guarantees religious freedom and Title VII of the Civil Rights Act of 1964 prohibits discrimination in all aspects of employment, including religion. Religion is broadly defined in Title VII to include all religious observances, practices, and sincerely held beliefs, even if they are unconventional. Employees do not have to belong to an organized religious sect to come under protection of this law.

The Supreme Court has defined religious belief as those that are "sincere and meaningful" and occupy a place in the life of an individual "parallel to that filled by the orthodox belief in God . . ."

Title VII provides a narrow exception for an employer engaged in religious activities to the extent that it may employ persons of a particular religion to perform services related to its religious purpose that are a *bona-fide* occupational qualification.

Action steps: In preparing to handle requests for religious accommodation, management should consider:

■ Developing and publicizing a policy regarding religious accommodation; for example, voluntary substitutions, job swaps, flexible scheduling, and using floating or optional holidays. If diversity training is offered, religion should be included.

■ Making supervisors and managers aware of Title VII precedent in this area, providing an avenue for complaints to be received and investigated before EEOC involvement, and encouraging with posters and training, an atmosphere conductive to a productive work experience.

SABOTAGE

Nature of the problem: Sabotage is the destruction or vandalism of company or employee property. It is a form of violence in the workplace. It can involve employee theft of office materials or overspending company monies. Vengeful employees have sabotaged computer files, erasing critical product information.

Issues to consider: Managers should consider the following in handling sabotage that affects the company's assets or employee property:

- An investigation should be mounted immediately, and information should be gathered by upper management with assistance from an outside investigator, if necessary. In serious cases, local police should be called and involved in the investigation. Undercover surveillance may be appropriate.

- Has the organization faced any significant change recently—a corporate downswing, the loss of a major customer, or the relocation of facilities? Sometimes employees will engage in sabotage to protect their turf. Employers should examine how well they communicated the need for change in advance. Sometimes it is a plain, destructive person who has found a place in the employer's workforce.

- Is computer access controlled? Sabotage of computer equipment and files can range from erasure of an important file to the destruction of documents and retrieval systems.

Applicable government regulations: The federal government's EEOC Guidelines on Sexual Harassment specify that "sabotaging a person's work" is part of a "hostile work environment," and the employer may be found to have violated these guidelines if sabotage is allowed to continue unchecked at the workplace. Criminal prosecution may be in order if sufficient evidence is gathered.

Action steps: Managers encountering cases of alleged sabotage should proceed with caution and be guided by an attorney:

■ What happened? Managers should document exactly what has been destroyed or damaged and take photographs of the damaged equipment or area. An insurance estimate should be obtained on the cost of returning the area or equipment to regular condition.

■ Who's at fault? In a few cases an employee may be caught engaging in the sabotage and should be turned over to the proper authorities. In other cases the rumor mill may provide information that investigators will want. If the facts substantiate it, firm, decisive action should be taken with the saboteur—which will send a message to other workers that the employer looks at such destructive activity seriously.

SEXUAL HARASSMENT

Nature of the problem: Sexual harassment can be regarded as a form of violence, usually against women. It can cause fatigue, exhaustion, stress, nervous disorders, sleeplessness, and hypertension in its victims.

Harassment can have a serious, negative effect on productivity and morale and result in absences and resignations, since some employees are unwilling to accept a negative work atmosphere.

Managers are in the forefront of enforcing a company's policy on harassment. An employer's greatest concern should be with managers who become aware of a problem and think that allegations of harassment will, given some time, just "go away." If managers are told of instances of sexual harassment and do nothing, they open themselves and the company to lawsuits.

Sexual harassment is defined by the Equal Employment Opportunity Commission (EEOC), the enforcing agency for complaints about the conduct, as "unwelcome sexual advances, requests for sexual favors, and other verbal or physical conduct of a sexual nature, when:

- Submission to such conduct is made either explicitly or implicitly a term or condition of an individual's employment, or

- Submission to or rejection of such conduct is used as a basis for employment decisions affecting individual, or

- It has the purpose or effect of unreasonably interfering with an individual's work performance or creating an intimidating, hostile, or offensive working environment."

A sexually hostile work environment can be created by:

- Telling off-color jokes

- Commenting on physical attributes

- Displaying sexually suggestive pictures

- Using demeaning or inappropriate terms

- Using indecent gestures

- Engaging in hostile physical conduct

- Discussing sexual activities

- Granting job favors to those who participate in consensual activities

- Using crude and offensive language

Remember that only unwelcome conduct is considered sexual harassment. Consensual dating, joking, and touching do not constitute harassment under federal law if they are not unwelcome or offensive to the persons involved.

Issues to consider: Managers faced with a complaint about harassment should take the complaint seriously and consider:

- The real issue in determining if the conduct is sexual harassment is whether the behavior is unwelcome, not whether the behavior is voluntary or involuntary.

- Both stories need investigating.

- Does the employer have a policy against sexual harassment that clearly communicates a method for complaints to be registered and promptly investigated?

- Does the workforce understand that there is a complaint process that they can use to register complaints of harassment?

- Both men and women can be the victims of sexual harassment, and either a man or a woman can be the harasser or the harassed.

- What if the immediate supervisor is the harasser? The complaint process should offer additional avenues to register complaints— upper level management and the human resources manager, in addition to the supervisor, to ensure reporting at any level of the organization.

Applicable government regulations: The Sexual Harassment Guidelines of Title VII require employers to maintain a workplace free of sexual harassment and prohibit a hostile work environment to exist. Many states also have laws prohibiting harassment in the workplace.

To determine whether behavior is severe or prevalent enough to create a hostile work environment, courts have considered the following factors:

- The frequency of the unwelcome discriminatory conduct

- The severity of the conduct

- Whether the conduct was physically threatening or humiliating, or merely an offensive utterance

- Whether the conduct unreasonably interfered with work performance

- The effect on the employee's psychological well-being

- Whether the harasser was a superior in the organization.

Action steps: Effective management of complaints about sexual harassment on the job are usually beyond the scope of an individual manager; it is up to senior management, and particularly the human resources professional, to develop policies and procedures for managers to investigate such complaints thoroughly and handle them expeditiously.

- The organization's published policy against sexual harassment should be widely communicated to supervisors and employees. The employer should provide a comprehensive list of categories of prohibited conduct. New employees should be made aware of the policy at orientation time and the policy should be reaffirmed from time to time in meetings and company publications. Newly appointed supervisors should be trained in the policy and what to do and what resources are available to assist a supervisor who encounters a harassment situation. Refresher training should be offered to all managers from time to time.

- Supervisors should be trained to take all sexual harassment complaints seriously. The supervisor is usually the first person to be told of a problem and should investigate the matter in a serious tone, taking a nonjudgmental, professional attitude and proceed to gather the necessary facts.

   The supervisor should not say that the complainant is being oversensitive. If a behavior is offensive to the complaining employee, that reaction should be taken seriously.

SEXUAL HARASSMENT

105

- The employee should be told that once an allegation of harassment is raised the company has an obligation to investigate the allegation. If the company is made aware of harassment and fails to investigate, it could be held liable for not preventing harassment in the workplace.

- The supervisor should gather facts and ask a few key questions: Has the employee asked the offending employee to stop the harassment? Except in the case of physical harassment, this should be the victim's first step.

- The supervisor should ask: What can I do to assist? Find out what the complainant's expectations are. Sometimes a complaint can be settled if the complaining employee simply wants an apology and a pledge not to repeat the action identified. While the supervisor cannot promise that the employee's name will not be released, reassurance should be given that the matter will be handled professionally and only those who are in a company position with a need to know will be part of the investigation.

- The supervisor should draw on resources such as senior level managers or the human resources department to assist the investigation. The victim should not be reassigned or disciplinary action taken against the perpetrator until the facts are in and a course of action decided on. The harasser and the victim should be informed of the decision.

- Hesitation can prove costly. The employee should be told approximately how long the investigation will take; if additional time is required, the employee should be so informed.

- Once the results of the investigation are in and an unacceptable act confirmed, the manager should be prepared to discipline fairly and swiftly. Follow established disciplinary procedures.

A physical assault probably warrants immediate suspension until an investigation is completed; the suspension may be converted to a termination at a later date should the facts justify such an action. Depending on the magnitude of the infraction, the employee's past work record and the remorse demonstrated during the investigation, the discipline may result in a transfer or termination of the guilty person. Courts will look at the adequacy of the remedy as well as the employer's belief that continued harassment was likely. Such a warning may be a good way to solve the problem so that the victim of the harassment can avoid contact with the person and the guilty party better understands the seriousness of his or her behavior.

- Should a complaint of harassment be settled short of termination, the manager should check with the complaining employee from time to time to reaffirm that the adverse conditions no longer exist. Also make clear to the offending employee the future consequences of misconduct of an associated nature.

- Ensure that a system is in place protecting all parties against adverse action or retaliation. A transfer might be a logical way to resolve a conflict between two employees, but it is better to transfer the harasser, not the victim. Be on the lookout for any retaliation by the harasser against the complaining employee.

SEXUAL HARASSMENT

107

STRESS

Nature of the problem: Stress can develop from problems on the job, personal problems away from work, or the individual's own personality, outlook on life, or lifestyle. Job stress can develop from excessive workloads, workstation crowding, noise, environmental air pollution, problems with a manager, or conflict with co-workers. All these can affect worker productivity and job quality. Sickness and depression may follow.

Issues to consider: Managers should consider the following elements when investigating what appears to be a stressed-out employee:

- How is the person's job performance affected?

- Has the employee identified work conditions that cause the stress?

- Has the employee developed a set of priorities on the job? Does the employee know his or her limits—how much she is required to do or produce or can do? Has the manager given direction on work priorities?

- A person under stress may be a candidate for an accident at work. A manager needs to be careful that such persons are not assigned to work that could result in injury.

- The side effects of medication prescribed for stress can vary with each person and may present safety implications on the job.

Applicable government regulations: A person with a mental stress condition may qualify for protection under the ADA.

Action steps: Managers who are advised by an employee that a stress condition exists can assist health care professionals as follows:

- Encourage the employee to discuss any job conditions that are causing the stress. Investigate the situation and take corrective action where appropriate.

■ Encourage physical exercise as a method to reduce stress. Encourage the employee to eat nutritious food and control consumption of stimulants such as alcohol, sugar, and caffeine. Corporate wellness programs, particularly, can help.

■ Services of an employee assistance program can help with referrals to trained psychologists.

Resources to assist: National Mental Health Association, 1021 Prince St., Alexandria, Virginia 22314; 1-800-969-6642. Ask for their free booklet on stress.

STRESS

109

TARDINESS

Nature of the problem: Tardiness is a form of absence from the job—arriving at the job late, leaving the job early for breaks or lunch, returning late to the job, or leaving the job before the end of the scheduled work day. In some companies these employees are called "early departures."

Absenteeism usually involves absence from work for an entire work day; tardiness can be more difficult to manage because the patterns of showing up on the job are irregular and often unpredictable.

Tardiness has a distressing effect on job morale, since other workers wonder why one person gets away with the tardiness when they are held to company standards of reporting to work on time. Investigation and action is needed by a manager.

Issues to consider: Managers should consider:

- Why is the person tardy? All sorts of reasons or excuses may be given, but the manager should emphasize that the person is needed on the job at the scheduled starting time. Absence from the workstation at scheduled times is like cheating or stealing time from the company.

- Are break times scheduled, or do employees relieve each other for breaks? The first policy is easier to manage; the latter is more difficult to supervise.

- What documentation system is used to show patterns of tardiness?

- If regular attendance is required on the job, is it listed as an essential job function? For example, a line mechanic's tardiness is a serious problem if that one person supports many line workers who must stand around if the mechanic doesn't show up on time.

- Is progressive discipline used to bring the matter of tardiness forcibly to the attention of the errant employee? Is discipline applied uniformly and without discrimination?

■ Were any mitigating factors involved in the tardiness? You may need to allow for extenuating circumstances.

■ Are the tardy persons bored with the job or not feeling appreciated and drifting in and out of work?

Applicable government regulations: The FMLA permits some absences, although it does not specifically cover tardiness.

Action steps: In assessing a problem of tardiness, managers should consider:

■ Employers should develop written attendance guidelines incorporating applicable provisions of the FMLA. These guidelines should also outline steps managers should take when employees are unable or unwilling to meet the prescribed guidelines. Employees need to see that the supervisor and the company are serious about absences.

■ Employers should publicize and communicate the policies to employees.

■ Managers should insist that any telephone calls reporting tardiness come directly to them or an immediate assistant. When the manager gets the calls they should ask what the problem is and when the person will report to the job. The manager's personal involvement will evidence strong interest in the problem.

■ The company should have a policy about being at the workstation for scheduled periods of work, and supervisors should follow up to be sure that the policy is enforced.

■ Company policy should require medical documentation for tardiness claiming illness or injury as a cause.

■ Managers should watch for patterns of tardiness. Off-the-job social events can cause tardiness the next work day.

■ Tardiness is often listed as an area for the application of progressive discipline. Be sure that any absences are not protected absences under the FMLA or the ADA

■ As a start to the discipline cycle, if necessary, the employee should be told that he or she is expected on the job on time and is not to leave the job until the designated quitting time.

TARDINESS

THEFT

Nature of the problem: A company's susceptibility to theft depends largely on what products it manufactures or service it provides, and how products are assembled, warehoused, and shipped. Consumer electronics, fragrances, precious metals, and high tech items are favorite targets for workplace thieves or outsiders who scout an employer's premises for theft opportunities. Thieves also go after company trade secret information, often found in computer storage files.

Managers should also realize that a small number of people are kleptomaniacs—with an inbred urge to steal—and others use the proceeds from workplace thefts for their personal gain.

Knowingly falsifying company documents or records is a form of theft.

Managers should never accuse an employee of theft. First conduct a complete investigation under the direction of an attorney. Information should be collected by a private security company—facts that the employer is prepared to prove in court.

As much as 2% of sales revenue is typically lost to employee theft. Theft by customers and outsiders adds to that figure. As a result, the problem stays unsolved, customers pay higher prices, and businesses suffer serious morale problems.

Issues to consider: In evaluating a problem of possible theft at the organization, a manager should consider:

■ Is the facility retail, wholesale, or manufacturing?

■ What is the product? A product that is easy to resell or trade will be in high demand on the street. A manufacturer of computers or a liquor warehouse has much more to be concerned about than a distributor of paper towels.

■ Do you know what you are losing? What type of inventory control system is in place, and how frequently are inventories taken and by whom? The first rule of loss prevention is to know what you have and to keep track of it.

 112

- What security controls are in place, if any? What is the state of fencing and exterior lighting at the facility? How is entry and exit to the facility controlled? What controls are in place for the removal of company product, company property, or employees' personal belongings from the facility?

- Are prospective new hires checked for substance abuse? Some employers also believe that the use of properly validated "honesty tests" help weed out potentially untrustworthy employees.

- Are employees allowed free exit and reentry at breaks or lunch times and access to their personal vehicles during the course of the shift?

- How are goods delivered to the facility, and who checks quantities and escorts service people from the premises? Are trash disposal areas inspected?

- Who checks inventories? What items are missing? Who has access to these areas?

- Is access to computers restricted?

- Have employees involved in cash or financial transitions or in purchasing activities been checked out or investigated? Are such employees bonded?

- Is a security guard service used?

Action steps: A facility security plan should include the following elements:

- Define stealing and communicate that definition to all employees. Make clear that all supplies, materials, and end products, including scrap, are company property and may not be removed from the premises.

- Are managers held to the same policy as employees? Written management permission should be required to remove any company property from the premises.

- Inventory controls should include locking up and caging items, taking inventory regularly, and rotating the responsibility for inventory taking. Surveillance cameras may help in some areas.

■ Control access to the facility—front, back, shipping and receiving docks, fencing, and exit and entry.

■ Valuable items should be locked up. Mechanics and technicians should be required to lock up company tools at the end of their shift.

■ Managers and employees should be made aware of the cost of theft to the business. All personnel need to know when there is a problem of loss and that the company looks on the loss seriously.

■ Know who you are hiring. Insist on fully completed employment application forms, and check out work performance with the applicant's former manager(s). If you can't get good information on the person's work experience, you may want to back away from the hire.

■ Computer access should be restricted with passwords and limited file access. Access codes should be changed regularly. Restrictions on each employee's computer access should be defined clearly.

■ Employees should know that any violation of company rules on theft and security will be grounds for termination and legal action. Many companies fire, rather than prosecute, employees who are caught stealing. The company avoids bad publicity and lawsuits by accused employees.

■ Investigation of any thefts should be handled by an attorney so that any information the employer receives will be protected by attorney-client privilege. All documents should be created in anticipation of future legislation or outside government agency review. Obtain guidance from the attorney before questioning an employee.

■ Polygraph testing is permitted, but only under very stringent rules.

UNSAFE WORK PRACTICES

Nature of the problem: A small number of employees (estimated at less than 5%) perform their jobs unsafely despite federal and state safety regulations and company safe working policies that mandate safe work practices.

Unsafe work practices may injure the employee or other workers, give a poor example to co-workers, and damage company equipment. There are several obvious indicators of unsafe work practices:

- Training in the safe way to perform a job is offered, but a few employees don't practice what they learn.

- The employee fails to wear the prescribed personal protective equipment such as eye or hearing protection.

- Machine guards are bypassed.

- Poor maintenance routines, such as neglecting to check out an electrical cord or a ladder before use, are practiced.

- The employee's immediate work area is a mess, with tripping hazards from poor housekeeping.

Any employee may be guilty of some of this behavior, but what supervisors should be seeking is patterns or continuance of the behaviors and failure to respond to correction.

Issues to consider: A manager who observes employees engaging in unsafe work practices should ask these questions:

- Has the organization established safe work practices for each job? Preparation of a job safety analysis for each job will help pinpoint safe—and unsafe—work practices.

- Are employees trained initially and retrained, if necessary, in safe work practices?

- Do managers and/or team leaders set a good example and correct any unsafe work practices observed?

■ Are employees involved in safety activities? Is "safety" dictated from above without employee involvement?

■ Is designated personal protective equipment available and in good working condition? Is its use required and enforced?

Any unsafe work practices should be stopped on the spot, and workers should be counseled and redirected. Approach the problem directly, rather than ignoring it, which will make it worse.

Applicable government regulations: OSHA requires training of employees in the safety requirements of their jobs under many of its standards. The General Duty Clause (Section 5 (a) 1) requires employers to provide "employment and a place of employment which are free from recognized hazards that are causing or likely to cause death or serious physical harm to employees. . . ." That same clause requires employees to comply with all occupational safety and health standards and all rules, regulations and orders issued under the Act. . . ."

Action steps: A manager can take several steps to achieve long-term correction in unsafe work practices:

■ Restate firmly what the correct work practices are and why they should be followed. Praise other aspects of the worker's performance, if appropriate, and restate the need for correcting the unsafe work practices. Tell how these practices can have a negative effect on other employees. Use visual reminders wherever possible and post them at work stations.

■ Make sure workers know the correct practices. Sometimes workers are unclear about the correct, safe way because training took place long ago or they weren't paying attention. Perhaps the procedures weren't explained in a way that they understand.

■ Managers should keep their tempers and avoid blame to prevent a defensive response. Managers should talk about the behavior they want to change, not the individual.

■ Encourage employees and tell them that you will check back in a few days to see how they are doing. Do follow-up to correct unsafe practices and get them back on track. Discipline may be required.

VIOLENCE, FIGHTING AND HORSEPLAY ON THE JOB

Nature of the problem: Most incidents of workplace violence result from robbery or other crime in a work setting; yet workplace attacks on the job are also an increasing problem.

An outburst on the job can be triggered by events such as a death or divorce in the family, financial problems, the advent of the holiday season, petty jealousies or disputes that escalate, or corporate changes such as layoffs.

Fighting at work is a form of violence and needs to have the same prompt managerial attention as an incident of violence. Horseplay on the job or "fooling around at work" is reckless behavior and can lead to violence (if action escalates) or injury, particularly if machinery or plant vehicles are nearby.

Issues to consider: Managers who want to prevent incidents of violence at the workplace should consider these issues:

■ Are reference checks conducted on prospective new employees? Courts have decided that an employer who does not check references carefully can be legally liable for hiring a violent employee. A key issue is the amount of contact the employee could have with the general public and the opportunity the job provides to injure others.

■ Potentially violent people are loners with few friends, exhibit violent behavior on occasions, express threats to specific persons and have a history of poor interpersonal relationships, abuse to others and firearms ownership. Not every person who fits this profile will commit an act of violence, and not every person who commits an act of violence will fit these indicators.

■ Supervisors should never meet alone with a potentially danger-ous employee and they should not attempt to psychoanalyze employees. The supervisors' role is to report errant behavior and

117

deterioration of work performance to the proper levels of management, receive guidance, and arrange for outside assistance as needed.

■ When employees fight, supervisors and co-workers may be tempted to try to separate the belligerents. They may succeed; however, one or both of the fighters may have a weapon on their person.

■ Are the services of an employee assistance program available to potentially violence-prone employees?

Applicable government regulations: OSHA includes a General Duty clause which charges employers with the responsibility of providing a workplace free from recognized hazards that are likely to cause death or serious injury. OSHA has charged some employers with laxity after incidents of workplace violence and issued penalties accordingly.

Action steps: The threat of violence will dictate the type of program needed:

■ Physical intervention should be the last resort in coping with a potentially violent person and should be handled by the police. A manager or co-worker should never come closer than five feet to an agitated worker.

■ Try to talk with the upset person and get them to sit down, which will help relax them.

■ The best place to start a violence prevention program is in the company's hiring procedures. Evaluate applicants carefully.

■ Establish a committee to focus on security of the building and employees and steps to be taken in a workplace emergency. If an emergency evacuation committee has already been established, that group can assume the functions of workplace security as well. It is wise to have representation from managers, workers, office staff, and production or service functions so that maximum input on security and safety issues can be gathered.

■ A security audit performed by the security committee and/or outside professional assistance is an important starting point. Among the materials reviewed should be the history of any incidents at the facility, control procedures for entry and exit, exterior fencing and lighting, and awareness training for managers and the safety committee.

■ Develop a policy of zero tolerance for sexual harassment, vandalism, intimidation, and horseplay. Develop the policies that managers should follow for discipline and suspension in such cases. Communicate the policy to the workforce that such incidents will not be tolerated.

While there is no foolproof way of insulating the workforce from violence, careful hiring practices and training managers and employees to respond effectively to potentially violent situations can make a substantial difference in the outcome of such events.

VIOLENCE, FIGHTING AND HORSEPLAY ON THE JOB

WORKPLACE DRESS CODES

Nature of the problem: Not every person employed wants or needs to come to work dressed in business attire, but what is appropriate workplace wear for the factory worker may not be suitable for the sales office or the laboratory. In some jobs, personal safety may dictate the type of personal attire or protective gear to be worn on the job. Customer relations or personal sanitation are also factors in dictating certain work attire on the job.

More organizations are relaxing their standards of what to wear to the job. Casual attire can be a morale booster and lowers status barriers at a time when many organizations are inviting greater employee involvement in their businesses.

Grooming standards such as dress, appearance, facial hair, and headgear policies may give rise to religious discrimination claims. The key inquiry will focus on the employer's business need for particular dress or appearance requirements. Removing facial hair, women mandated to wear pants on the work site, and the removal of yarmulkes are examples of dress and appearance requirements that have been challenged.

Some organizations have provided uniforms for their employees, smocks for managers and laboratory or technical personnel, and different-colored hard hats for supervisors, first aid, and safety personnel.

A 1996 survey by the Society for Human Resource Management (SHRM) of 505 human resource managers showed that 90% of the companies allowed office workers to wear casual clothing to work, either regularly or on special occasions. A similar survey in 1992 indicated that 63% held that policy.

Issues to consider: Line managers should try to determine company policies on standard dress codes for work. Here are some thoughts in developing a dress code policy:

- What image does the business want to present? That image should reflect business needs, the image the employer wants to present, or the safety and security needs of the business.

■   Consider the job. Dress codes for a bank's platform officer or a teller who meets the public every day may need to be more polished than the staff back in the computer room. The kind of attire appropriate for the front office of a manufacturing facility is usually unnecessary for the production floor, where the work environment can involve dust, grease, and oil. On the other hand, safe work attire for a welder includes a head shield, heavy protective gloves, and a heavy-duty work apron.

■   How do employees feel about such a change? Their input should be invited so that the ultimate policy is self-regulated by employees.

Applicable government regulations: Employers have the right to set reasonable standards for dress in their workforces, and the courts have generally supported such policies as long as employees are informed of the restrictions when they are hired or when the new policy comes into effect.

Managers should not develop dress standards that are discriminatory to one gender—for example, allowing women but not men to wear earrings. A grooming policy that is enforced differently against men and women can lead to liability for gender bias.

OSHA requires the use of personal protective equipment in some work assignments. Specific OSHA regulations should be reviewed with this in mind.

Action steps: Many business managers have acceded to employee requests for more leisurely work attire by asking themselves:

■   Is formal business attire required for every position? Wearing casual attire can be looked on as a perk—allowing employees to save money by buying clothing they can use on workdays and weekends.

■   Human resources managers should coordinate the dress code policy so that it reflects business necessity. Dress code standards must be nondiscriminatory and applied uniformly to all employees regardless of race, color, sex, national origin, or religion.

■   Employers should invite employees to contribute to dress code policy because it should accommodate employee interests and desires. Acceptable and unacceptable attire should be illustrated and explained.

■ Managers also need to be involved in policy development and approval so that they can set the example on the new dress code.

■ The policy should outline the style of dress or wear for the job, responsibilities of employees in keeping their attire neat, and the possible consequences for violations of the policy. Employees who do not conform to the policy need to be counseled and disciplined, if necessary.

YOUNG WORKERS

Nature of the problem: Laws at the federal, state, and local level dictate the minimum age at which young people are permitted to work. The laws also usually list the ages at which young persons may not work and what jobs they may not perform.

According to the federal Bureau of Labor Statistics, more than 4.5 million young people (those age 18 and under) work at summer and part-time jobs while at school, and their accident rates are higher than adults who work in similar jobs.

Adolescents in their first job may have less experience in recognizing hazards and, as part of typical teenage curiosity, are more likely to take chances. Therefore, training in the proper methods and safe use of tools and equipment is essential. Many young people are shy, don't want to appear "stupid" to peers, and may be reluctant to ask questions.

The leading causes of death to youths on the job are motor vehicle accidents, machine and tractor accidents, electrocution, homicides, and falls. Injuries on the job range from burns associated with food service work, cuts from opening cardboard cartons in stores, sprains and strains due to overexertion, eye injuries from the debris thrown by lawnmowers, and hand and finger injuries from food slicer and car wash equipment.

Issues to consider: Managers who supervise young workers should understand the federal, state, and local labor laws that apply to these workers. Do not assign these young people to prohibited occupations.

Companies with a human resource department often screen candidates and do not present applicants to a manager unless they are old enough for the job. Some employers insist on a work permit.

Managers facing performance problems with young workers should consider:

- Is the person allowed to perform this job? State and federal law designate certain jobs where young persons are not permitted to work.

■ Is the schedule of hours permitted by state law? Some states limit the hours of work and nighttime hours that young persons are permitted to work.

■ If money handling is involved, what security controls are in place?

■ Is training provided and assistance available through a job instructor or mentor?

Applicable government regulations: Regulations at the federal, state, and local level dictate the age at which young persons are permitted to work and occupations they are not permitted to perform. A local human resources department should be aware of these restrictions and present only those job candidates to the hiring manager whose employment and occupation is permitted by law.

Action steps: A first job is the first step in the world of work for many young people, and it is essential that young workers get a solid foundation of what is expected of them as employees. The first job can set the tone for the rest of their lives.

Managers who feel they have a work performance problem with young workers should consider these steps:

■ Be satisfied that the young person is permitted to work, permitted to work on the particular job, and permitted to work the schedule of hours the manager wants. Check with the local high school about cooperative programs, since the coordinators know state and local restrictions.

■ Provide safety orientation for the young worker.

■ Designate a job instructor, mentor, or co-worker who will train the person, correct any unsafe work habits, and generally watch out for the young employee on the job.

■ Young people often need encouragement in learning and performing what for many may be a first job in industry. They need friendly encouragement, redirection at times, and praise for work done well. If work is not done well, the young person, like any other employee, should be counseled and redirected. Some times a transfer to a less demanding job may be required.

■ The manager should follow up to be sure that the young person is performing the job correctly and safely.

PART

III

MODIFYING PERFORMANCE

CHAPTER 6

COMMUNICATING EFFECTIVELY WITH EMPLOYEES

Good employee communication requires keeping people apprised of changes involving their work and advising employees about the company and industry changes before the information leaks to outsiders or the media. Communication should be a two-way street: employees should be able to share their opinions and comments, ideas and input. As basic as those precepts sound, they are too often forgotten by a busy management group.

At the new hire stage, communication involves well-planned orientation sessions, clear benefit information, an up-to-date employee handbook, and a planned introduction to the job through instruction and supervision by managers and mentors.

Once the new employee is operational, another set of communication tools comes into play. Many organizations have crew meetings or regular department get-togethers where information and mutual concerns are aired. Other organizations hold staff meetings where managers discuss trends such as the month-end financial statements. Some employers have quarterly or semiannual "state of the business" meetings where senior managers update employees on business trends and problems and unveil impending changes in the business or personnel policies.

Perhaps the most personal method of on-the-job communication about work performance are the interchanges between supervisor and employee at the workstation. Most of these aren't fancy or formal. Communications usually takes place in short, stand-up discussions at the workstation, but managers might sit down with the worker in the supervisor's office to review performance and suggest changes or corrective procedures. These discussions take place every hour of every work day in the workplaces of America, and the vast majority of these interchanges are effective.

More formal workplace communication also takes place in performance evaluation sessions, where the supervisor reviews the employee's job performance and achievement of job goals.

When carried out properly, performance evaluations can be a management tool for minimizing the effect of declining job performance. Formal performance evaluations normally summarize the discussion in writing; the employee is invited to add comments and asked to sign the evaluation. The evaluation session should result in a continuing of strong performance or the correction of poor performance.

GOAL SETTING

Performance appraisals often include goal setting—where supervisor and employee jointly plan job or work improvement objectives for a certain period of time. These are usually specific job responsibilities— "complete installation of new stamping press by January 31" or "learn new word processing equipment within three months and convert all files to it within five months." Goal achievement is then reviewed periodically, perhaps quarterly, to assess progress. Revisions may then be made to the goals and the completion dates.

Coaching

Coaching is king on the athletic fields of America, but it has achieved less prominence in the workplaces of America. Sometimes called redirection, reinstruction, or counseling, coaching means setting employees straight on the "right way to do it" and on the track of job success.

Managers may coach, but sometimes they use trained help—an assistant, a mentor, a designated substitute, or a job instructor—who can spend more time with the particular employee.

Implementing Change

Persons at work become accustomed to a routine—the same faces, the same kind of work, the same supervisors, the same co-workers. In such situations there is little change.

Resistance is the most common side effect of change. Most people don't like change and resist it—unless they are told that a change is forthcoming, it is explained to them, and they have opportunities to ask questions and provide feedback about the change. Resistance tells a manager that employees feel the change.

Some people will accept change as positive or even necessary. Others will resist change. Fully half of the work unit will sit on the fence to see what happens.

Education is the first step in introducing change. That's why it's so important to explain to employees the logic that drives the change.

Describe how industry trends, sales needs, or tougher quality standards require a change—and here are the details of the change. Explanations won't melt all the resistance, but they should swing most of the workers to understand and support the reason for change.

If major changes are in the offing, give as much time to planning the communication as you do to carrying out the communication. Be prepared to hit hard with the announcement—in the first few sentences—so that your people realize that major changes are afoot. That initial message should be so convincing that even the fence sitters realize that you are determined to make the changes stick because of the rationale that you unfold.

After explaining the reasons for the change, specify how it will affect the work group, on an individual basis if possible. People will want to know: "How will this affect me?" The best way to resolve employees' uncertainty is to tell them the truth as quickly as possible, even if it means telling people what they don't want to hear. Sooner is better than later.

Repeat what you say. People get distressed, think about themselves, and forget what they heard. As people question the need for change, they forget the logic behind the change and must be reminded of it. Change requires leadership and even cheerleading so that it overcomes resistance or apathy.

Good communication takes time and effort. There's a direct correlation between the quality of communication and how much resistance is involved in the intended change.

The Disciplinary Interview

The disciplinary interview is another employee communication tool, although usually regarded as a negative one. Many supervisors avoid resolving performance problems through disciplinary interviews. Most managers hope poor performance will improve spontaneously so that no action need be taken. Sometimes friendship prevents a supervisor from telling an employee that improvement is necessary. However, when positive communication and corrective steps have not improved the work performance of an employee, most companies insist that a formal disciplinary process be commenced, unless the facts of the situation warrant immediate suspension or termination.

Using Media to Communicate

Management often communicates to employees through the printed word. Payroll stuffers now occur only rarely since wages are often paid by direct deposit, and bulletin boards, once a common communications medium, tend to get cluttered with government required notices. Suggestions systems and idea awards are still popular in many companies where employees suggest improvements, and awards are based on the value of that suggestion.

The core communication instrument is the company policy manual, which guides managers on how the company wants to relate to employees. The employee handbook, another communication tool, should mirror policies found in the policy manual.

Letters to employees are used occasionally to convey important information to employees at their home address. If used sparingly and reserved for important communications, these more personalized methods can gain favorable reaction and understanding in the home setting where family members also read the communication.

Tips for Good (Employee) Communication

If you want to get your message across to workers:

■ Make employee communication a principal management objective. Support the spoken words of supervisor to employee with messages printed and video media. When honest and straightforward communication is a way of life, employees will focus on work objectives.

■ Communicate honestly. The honesty of your communication determines what you are worth in the minds of your employees—the culture and character of the company and its ethics.

■ Communicate quickly. Don't let the grapevine speak for you. Keeping employees informed on matters that affect their jobs, the department, and the company will bolster motivation and job performance.

■ Talk in workers' terms. Fancy management jargon or engineering-technical words may be considered pompous and alienating by many. Tell employees the changing news by the third sentence of the announcement, then fill in the details.

■ Be prepared to share bad news. At some time you will have to tell your employees about some aspect of the business that affects them negatively—the closing of a department, the loss of a large customer, a dangerous safety situation. Get the worst information out. If the incident turns out to be less serious, you and your employees will be relieved. Bad news is never pleasant, but it is worse when it is badly delivered.

continued on next page

continued from previous page

■ Invite questions. This is frightening for some managers, but it is the only way to two-way communication. The presenter should be knowledgeable and able to field questions. Present more information than is necessary; reword what is happening at the midpoint of the presentation; then restate and summarize at the end.

In some cases, "I don't know at this point" is an acceptable response; also acceptable is "Let me check into that and I'll get back to you." End a session like this by saying, "As we get more information we will communicate it to you promptly either through a meeting like this or through your managers."

■ Consider special circumstances. In some cases where litigation may result, it is wise to read from a prepared statement approved by company counsel. In other cases, it may be prudent to hand out a summary that follows very closely what was said. Such a step limits the chance of misunderstandings. When many workers are affected, repeat the message exactly through your electronic mail system; offer a toll-free number and invite employee questions.

Newsletters and company magazines are still used to bring the "company story" to employees and their families. Pictures of employees at work are always well received.

High-tech communications have also entered the employee communications field. Some facilities have large-screen television sets where company or facility news is broadcast, production progress charted by the hour, and new sales orders listed. Nobody likes a TV set on for eight hours steadily, so frequent repeats of the information or 'hourly updates' are better used to attract attention.

The Internet has also become a communications tool for business, particularly organizations with widespread locations. A message entered at one work station can be broadcast by electronic mail to every person in the network.

Voice response systems are used by benefits departments to answer questions from employees about frequently asked benefit questions or to reallocate investments in 401(k) plans.

Video conferencing allows persons working in different locations to have face-to-face contact without incurring high costs or losing valuable time to travel.

Some far-thinking employers realize that it is difficult at times to flesh out true employee feelings about their jobs and the organization that employs them. Too often the silence is deafening. A few companies hire third-party organizations to collect comments, anonymously, from employees. It gives employees the chance to expose inefficiencies, attack emerging problems early in the cycle, and vent their feelings about the job to high levels in the company.

Employee participation and involvement are popular concepts in business these days. Employees need knowledge and information to do this best.

7

WHEN IT DOESN'T WORK OUT

If the manager displays good leadership techniques and the employee displays good motivation, most performance problems can be overcome and performance improved. This is the positive thrust of this book.

But not every performance problem can be overcome. Sometimes companies and workers part ways—the employee will quit, the employee may be terminated, the supervisor will leave, or the company will move away or go out of business. Not every person is suited for every company, nor is the culture of every company attractive to every worker.

One of the key responsibilities of a supervisor is managing employee performance fairly and legally, to administer the company's work rules and to confront problems when necessary. A series of discipline steps may be required if performance slips. Redirection, counseling, discipline, and termination processes are central to overcoming most performance problems.

The Quit or Resignation

In most cases when an employee resigns, voluntary termination is straightforward—the employee didn't like the work, had problems with the commute, didn't like the supervisor or co-workers, or found the pay inadequate for the work. (Note how some of these factors could have been avoided by using a thorough selection process recommended in Chapter 4.)

Some leave work, do not give notice, do not return to the job, and mail in a note asking to have any pay forwarded to them.

Layoffs

Many employees may be laid off when business activities are reduced or facilities closed. Sometimes poorly performing employees are pushed out under the guise of a business reduction or a layoff.

The handling of group layoffs requires careful planning, superb communication to workers, and some measure of assistance to those who are separated from the organization. Layoffs need to be handled with great care and employees involved treated with dignity.

If a large layoff is involved, confidential planning should go into the project. Work out plans so that longer-service employees can take advantage of transfers, demotions, and retraining provisions.

Federal, state, and local law needs to be reviewed, since the federal WARN Act (Worker Adjustment and Retraining Act) requires advance notice to persons affected by large staff cutbacks. Federal Title VII provisions prohibit creating an "adverse impact" on minorities and women by laying them off in disproportionate numbers. Some state laws also dictate protections in the case of layoffs, and these statutes need to be checked out.

Laid-off workers should be notified formally and individually about the reason for the layoff, the effective date, continuation of medical insurance coverage through COBRA, what efforts the company will make to find them employment in other units of the organization, and what job-finding assistance, if any, will be offered the departing employees.

Most laid-off employees will have to find new jobs. Some companies help terminating employees with transition assistance until they are employed elsewhere. In addition to government-required (but self-paid) medical insurance coverage, additional insurance continuation may also be provided. Severance or termination pay may be offered. Increasingly, organizations that terminate many employees offer outplacement assistance, which can be as basic as resume preparation to a full job-seeking assistance that involves interviewing skills and networking.

THE NECESSITY FOR A FORMAL DISCIPLINE PROCESS

Most employees want to perform at or above standards of productivity, quality, and service. However, every organization has a few employees who do not perform well and must be dealt with so that work morale and the efficiency of good performers is not dragged down.

Management should consider the following when developing a discipline process:

- The infraction should be handled promptly—immediately after the incident or, if time is needed to investigate, within 24 hours of the incident. Lateness in responding may be interpreted as approval of the action.

    If the incident is serious, suspend the employee (with or without pay, depending on company policy) for a short time, pending results of an investigation. In the final step before termination, some employers provide "decisional leave"—one day off with pay. The employee is asked to return after the paid day off with a written plan to amend behavior and stay with the company, or to resign.

- If management is not sure of any facts or information, investigate. The courts tend to look to the fairness and adequacy of an investigation and may penalize a company that has not investigated a complaint. An employer who knows or should know of sexual harassment, and does not thoroughly investigate and rectify the situation, faces the potential for substantial liability.

- Disciplinary interview sessions should be held in a private office or meeting room. The employee should never be embarrassed in front of others.

- Management representatives should establish a positive tone for the disciplinary hearing and conduct it in a sensitive and considerate manner. The employee should be asked to describe his or her side of the incident and suggest how to improve the situation. Management representatives should explain how the incident affected the company co-workers, and the individual.

137

■ The supervisor should emphasize the positive results that a change in behavior can bring. Suggest a follow-up session in a few days to discuss any suggestions developed in the meeting.

■ Document that a counseling or a disciplinary interview took place after the meeting. If discipline is required for several employees, resolve the worst cases first.

In some sensitive investigations, it may be important to have another person, preferably another manager, involved in the investigation or as a witness during the interview.

In a sensitive investigation (involving theft, for example), managers should consult with in-house counsel or an experienced outside employment attorney before starting an investigation. If the investigation is conducted at the direction of an attorney, the information may be considered privileged and confidential in the event of a lawsuit.

In the case of employee theft or criminal misconduct, the employer may decide to pursue the matter in civil or criminal courts. However, exercise extreme caution in conducting such investigations or in starting legal action, since overzealous or unfounded charges may subject the employer to liability for malicious prosecution, defamation, and invasion of privacy.

The Manager's Role in Discipline

A key role of a supervisor is a willingness and ability to confront employees with performance problems and take appropriate corrective action. Careful, specific, and documented action is more likely to improve the employee's work performance and decreases the employer's exposure to employment discrimination and wrongful discharge claims.

When a manager does a poor job in administering discipline, the results can be costly. The company becomes liable to lawsuits; moreover, morale and productivity among employees not subject to discipline may suffer. Supervisors who conduct discipline and termination sessions without good cause and sensitivity could be held personally liable by the courts and face assessment of damages.

Managers need assistance from upper management or the human resources professional in investigating facts surrounding employee misconduct, illegal activity in the workplace, or behavior that is detrimental to efficiency at the job site. However, it is the supervisor's responsibility to extend and apply discipline—not the personnel professional.

Disciplinary matters involving employees require due process—a protection of the U.S. Constitution. The complaining employee and the accused should both be heard. The manager must be open-minded until all facts are in. Consult with the company's attorney so that the investigation and subsequent action can have professional guidance.

Other Management Members Can Help

In most organizations, the manager of an employee with a performance problem doesn't have to go it alone. Other managers can provide guidance or help in the disciplinary process.

Upper level managers, including the manager's supervisor, can provide comments, suggestions, and perhaps a more detached, objective view of what happened and what remedy should be applied.

The on-site expert on disciplinary matters is often the personnel professional or human resources manager. That person should be familiar with federal, state, or local laws that may affect the discipline about to be applied and should also be able to assist with any investigation required.

The human resources professional should be the company officer assigned to evaluate whether written or informal company policies have been followed in the investigation of the incident and intended disciplinary processes. In fact, in many companies the human resources professional is charged with the responsibility of overviewing disciplinary and termination actions before such actions are taken.

THE MANNER OF TERMINATION

The manner in which an employee is terminated often has a great deal of influence on whether the employee files a charge or lawsuit against the organization.

A senior manager or the human resources manager should review the situation—ideally, in advance—and be satisfied that the termination action:

- Abides by federal and state legislation

- Follows company procedures on discipline or termination

- Meets company and legal procedural requirements in terms of final wage payments, vacation pay, and coverage under laws such as federal COBRA coverage, and any state extensions of that coverage

■ The interview is handled professionally and the employee is treated with dignity

Input From Exit Interviews

If the selection processes recommended in Chapter 4 are carried out effectively, the number of quits and terminations should be low. But when people quit, does management get to know the real reason?

Management usually knows the reason when they have to take disciplinary action and terminate an employee. In voluntary terminations, management does not always find out, since some employees fear that telling the truth would jeopardize recommendations or references. Accurate feedback from those leaving offers a prime opportunity to gain views on employment conditions in your company.

It is a sensible policy to require an exit interview with every person terminating—involuntary or otherwise—which can be weaved into the session when the employee returns to pick up a last pay check or to remove personal belongings. Some companies mail a survey to an employee who has already terminated to determine the reasons for leaving.

Responses to exit interviews do not exactly audit work satisfaction, since some persons have an axe to grind. Yet, a well-done exit interview can reflect the effectiveness of the organization's selection processes.

Avoiding Discrimination Charges and Lawsuits

Federal, state, and local legislation affects the day-to-day operation of a business and the employees who work there. Line and staff managers need to understand the basics of these laws—how they apply to the work setting, the enforcement agency involved, the range of penalties, and the statute of limitations to file a claim. Ignorance of the law does not permit a company to break it.

Most states have enacted laws covering employment-related matters and employee safety and health on the job. Some state laws almost duplicate the federal provisions, but managers need to become familiar with state laws affecting their businesses, since many of the state laws provide protection to employees which exceed requirements of the federal laws.

The EEOC or state-level fair employment practice agencies enforce discrimination law. The employee files the charge in writing with the proper agency, the employer is notified and defends the action by trying to prove a business necessity for its conduct. Managers applying discipline should understand the "no retaliation" provisions of many laws.

Taking preventive action. In any employment relationship, some problems will occur. How problems are handled affects a company's risk of being drawn into expensive litigation. When encountering an employee relations problem, the manager should ask these questions:

- What does the manager expect from the employee? The manager should state what performance level is expected and the corrective action that will ensue if it is not achieved.

- Does the company have a written policy or a consistent informal practice on particular personnel actions or problems such as sexual harassment or layoffs?

- Has the matter been investigated properly? The manager should try to determine what happened and what deviations there were from normal workplace behavior.

- Is there a company policy on progressive discipline, and have the progressive steps been taken up to this point? If company procedures require written documentation by either the supervisor or employee, have these steps been completed?

- Has the employee complaint been investigated? Supervisors have the initial responsibility to investigate complaints and report to the employee.

Legal Liability

Company executives and managers are routinely named these days as defendants in government charges or court cases filed by present and former employees who feel they have been discriminated against or unjustly treated. A few courts hold managers personally liable for their own acts of discrimination and for the acts of other managers and workers of which the managers have knowledge.

Under the law, executives, managers, and supervisors are often regarded as "agents" of the employer. For example, under Title VII of the Civil Rights Act of 1964, the term "employer" includes someone with 15 or more employees and any agent of that person, which includes managers and supervisors of the employer. The Fair Labor Standards Act defines an employer to include any person "acting directly or indirectly in the interest of the employer in relation to the employee." That broad definition would also include most managers and supervisors.

Business liability insurance normally protects officers and agents, but insurance does not usually cover any intentional acts, punitive damages, or criminal liability. If the manager acts outside his or her sphere of responsibility, the insurance coverage may not apply. Criminal liability is generally based on a reckless disregard for safety and not merely negligence. If a manager intentionally ignores warning signs, he or she can be held to have a reckless disregard.

Some state statutes carry criminal penalties if workers' rights are violated. For example, in many states, a terminated employee is entitled to final wages on the next business day after termination—not on the next regular payday. Some states require that new employees be informed in writing of their rate of pay, hours of work, and wage payment schedule at the time of hire.

Managers and supervisors need not be lawyers, but they must understand current legal requirements and what can happen in litigation.

MAKING A U-TURN

What does an employer do if an employee who has quit changes his or her mind and wants to return? There's a temptation to invite good workers to return promptly. But before that is done, the following should be considered:

- Has the supervisor already placed another person in the vacated job or promised the job to another person already employed? Bringing the person back may cause more morale problems with present staff than it is worth.

- How often do employees quit, then return in a few days? Management needs to sense the likelihood that returning employees will give others the idea to "try a new job and if it doesn't work you can always come back here."

Some companies tell terminated employees with good work records that they will certainly be considered for any new jobs that occur and that they will be placed on a preferred hiring list.

MAINTAINING EQUILIBRIUM

Supervising others on the job is not always an easy responsibility. The mark of an able manager is a person who can give clear direction, provide assistance and redirection to tasks, and still offer a work atmosphere that encourages cooperation and achievement of the organization's production, quality, service, and cost goals.

Supervisors are people, too, and personal feelings can easily detract from the objective handling of a counseling or discipline situation. At times it is difficult to keep personal feelings away from the conduct of business, but it must be done if the supervisor is to lead others.

Enhancing Goodwill in the Workplace

Most employees want to help achieve the goals of the company. The few who do not must be redirected so that they, too, can help achieve the purpose for which they are employed.

Just a few poor performers can detract from the positive efforts of a department or business unit and pull down the productive efforts of others. That's why the good work efforts of most of the people must always take precedence over those few who are unable or unwilling to meet workplace objectives. Good employees need to have their efforts rewarded with merit increases, production bonuses, and recognition. Those steps help keep that productive "engine" moving along the track of organization success.

Low achievers often require substantial amounts of the supervisor's time with efforts at redirection, reinstruction, mentoring, counseling and, if necessary, formal disciplinary processes. It may seem out of balance at times, but if poor performance is allowed to continue unchecked, it will soon depress the group's performance.

Supervisors should not forget that they have power over those who report to them. Supervisors control work assignments, promotions, transfers, merit increases, and—within the framework of a company's policies and the law—the right to terminate. That authority, properly exercised, gives the supervisor power—and leadership rights and responsibilities—over workers that should allow him or her to take charge. The supervisor's challenge in resolving performance problems is the ability to keep calm under pressure and find solutions that work.

Take your time. Don't rush into a performance improvement situation. Some supervisors put a lot of pressure on themselves to solve the situation fast. A sense of urgency is fine, but managers should make sure that the pressure of time is real and necessary.

A PERSPECTIVE ON A MANAGER'S JOB

A general manager in the chemicals industry with more than 100 direct and indirect supervisors and managers reporting to him viewed a manager's job as:

- An adviser who supplies useful and helpful information to the employee so that the employee, to the largest degree possible, can carry out the job without minute direction.

- A communication expert who tells the story of good work performance to upper management, co-workers, and new hires in the organization. If no one hears about your good work, that good work can go unrecognized or unrewarded.

 144

Keep Your Cool

Supervisors are people, too, and they can't be expected to stay calm all the time, particularly when dealing with a repeatedly errant employee. If you vent your anger and need to recover, here are some suggestions on how to do it gracefully:

■ Apologize. There's nothing that will calm the waters more quickly than the open statement, "I'm sorry. Please forgive me. I shouldn't have said that."

■ Allow a few seconds for tempers to cool, then proceed with the discussion. If you're still angry, adjourn the session and reconvene at a later time. Don't postpone the session too long—the errant employee may think he has the upper hand.

■ A constructive critic who tells employees directly and specifically where substandard performance has occurred and what needs to be done to upgrade performance to acceptable levels.

■ A cheerleader who encourages subordinates to do good work and to support and encourage when setbacks are encountered.

When an Employee Goes Over Your Head

What does a supervisor do when an employee goes over the supervisor's head to the supervisor's boss? Reprimanding the employee will accomplish little.

Most employees don't want to go over their supervisor's head and would like to try to work out things with their immediate boss. but if it happens here are some suggestions on what to do:

■ When you find out about it (probably from your manager), discuss the matter and decide how you will handle the employee's original complaint. Be certain that your manager supports the course of action in resolving the complaint and what you will tell the employee about the complaint, including that in future the employee is to come to you, the immediate supervisor, not your manager, with problems.

■ Tell the employee that you are aware of the situation and that you have talked with the manager.

■ Start over. Get the employee's version of what the problem is to be sure that you have all the facts, opinions, and feelings in the situation.

■ Let the employee know that you will investigate the matter (if that is necessary) and what, if anything, will be done. If the answer must be "no," state it clearly and politely and the reasons for the decision. Reaffirm any company policies in support of your decision.

If one of your staff members bypasses you, it may be time to do some self-analysis. A supervisor should ask: "Am I as accessible as I should be? Do my direct reports see me as approachable? How can I get better information so that I get first crack at solving these problems?" Introspection should provide answers to the problem of the occasional employee who goes around you.

A BALANCED WORKING RELATIONSHIP

At times it may seem that the small number of employees who need redirection are overwhelming the supervisor's attention. This is a big challenge, especially for the new supervisor who may have inherited a department with some difficult employees.

These trying situations bring out the best qualities in a supervisor— the ability to provide sustained leadership to the productive work of good employees, yet allocate time to redirect those who are not working up to standard or potential.

If a supervisor can't get through to the problem employee, perhaps a statement such as "Are you willing to work with me until we find a solution that meets both our needs?" may get you over the hump and on the road of redirection. Agreement on a collaborative approach allows you to continue the communication and problem solve with dignity and integrity.

Time to Relax

The best cures for anxiety and fear are rest and relaxation. Try scheduling time each day—perhaps at the end of lunch and certainly after work—for just plain relaxing. Relaxation will put you in a state of mind in which you will be more open to taking steps towards regaining balance.

Enhancing Morale

What makes for an enthusiastic workforce where morale is high? Important ingredients are expansion of the business, a strong sales picture, opportunity for advancement for the workers, and a happy life on the job.

Morale is high when employees share a positive sense of spirit and are willing to help organizations achieve their goals—that is, if they understand what the goals are. Too often rank-and-file employees don't have the vaguest idea what those goals are.

THE PAYOFF

Organizations that have developed a managed approach to resolving employee performance problems can turn around people with performance problems. Most of these employees have valuable experience, knowledge, and job training—qualities that are costly to replace.

Over time, too, supervisors' own performance improves as they get better at monitoring, measuring performance, counseling, and coaching employees.

Good managers are supportive managers. They encourage their employees to speak their minds, try out new approaches to work, and display energy and imagination. They accept occasional mistakes and even failure.

In most situations, a supervisor who leads good employees well, yet attends to those whose performance needs extra management, will over time see results. Production or service statistics will improve; quality and customer complaints should decline. Absenteeism and complaints should decline. And generally, employees who feel that they have been fairly treated are less likely to write grievances, file charges, or take the employer to court.

Good supervisors should be rewarded with merit increases, bonuses, or year-end incentive payments. Successful supervisors are sought out by fledgling supervisors who can benefit from their experience. And perhaps the greatest compliment of all is the supervisor who receives commendation and promotions from higher levels of management.

A P P E N D I X

Following is a job description of a typical manager or supervisor in business.

DEPARTMENT MANAGER JOB DESCRIPTION

Job Function

Takes charge of an operating shift to produce a product or provide a service in line with company product specifications and quality goals.

Principal Responsibilities

1. Develops among assigned personnel a consciousness of the need for teamwork to attain department objectives.

2. Reviews the daily production or service schedule for the department to plan work and personnel assignments for the shift.

3. Supervises and directs personnel in performing operations according to sound operating principles and company policies and procedures.

4. Anticipates and determines causes of delays in operations or service functions and takes appropriate corrective action to meet schedules.

5. Reports promptly to manager when delays occur; estimates time of delay and when operations will be resumed.

6. Directs personnel in the receipt of materials and supplies compared to quantities ordered and quality of specifications and advises purchasing department of deviations.

7. Enters required information in department computer; sends and receives electronic mail affecting department's operations.

8. Contacts engineering and maintenance departments for required repair work on shift and forwards a maintenance requisition for time and materials used.

9. Reviews defect bin at end of each shift and authorizes rework or scrapping of materials.

10. Studies operations where cost standards are not being met to determine causes and to apply corrective measures. Draws on staff department input such as industrial engineering, accounting, or human resources to assist as needed.

11. Interviews applicants, presented after screening by human resources department, for department jobs. With department job instructor and safety committee member, conducts orientation of new hires and their safety training on the job.

12. Conducts probationary and annual performance evaluation of each department employee and recommends performance increases, retraining, transfer, or termination.

13. Applies company employee relations policies in all dealings with employees.

14. Gives leadership to good housekeeping in the department.

15. Conducts month-end physical inventory of raw materials, supplies, and finished goods.

Qualifications

- In-company job experience as an above-average operator or line mechanic

- Strong personal leadership and communications abilities

- Junior college training in mechanical technology or equivalent manufacturing industry experience

- Willingness to work rotating shifts (every four weeks at this time)

ABOUT THE AUTHOR

Neville C. Tompkins of Cedar Run, New Jersey, is a human resources consultant and writer who has had extensive experience in line and staff positions in industry, helping resolve hundreds of the problems faced by managers for whom this book is intended.

He was formerly a director of human resources at the corporate offices of Continental Can Co., Inc. and he has achieved certification as a senior professional in human resources (SPHR), the highest professional designation in the human resources field.